DATE DUE

NOV 2 6 1993	
FEB - 7 1995	
DEC - 5 1996	
NOV 1 5 1998	
NOV 1 3 1999	
OCT 1 6 2000	
NOV 1 1 2000	
NOV 2 5 2000	

BRODART   Cat. No. 23-221

Dual-Career Marriage
A System in Transition

Dual-Career Marriage
A System in Transition

Lisa R. Silberstein

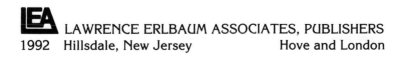

LAWRENCE ERLBAUM ASSOCIATES, PUBLISHERS
1992   Hillsdale, New Jersey   Hove and London

Lawrence Erlbaum Associates, Inc., Publishers
365 Broadway
Hillsdale, New Jersey 07642

Library of Congress Cataloging-in-Publication Data

Silberstein, Lisa R.
    Dual-career marriage : a system in transition / Lisa R.
  Silberstein.
        p.   cm.
    Includes bibliographical references and index.
    ISBN 0-8058-0712-8
    1. Dual-career families—United States.   I. TITLE.
    [DNLM: 1. Employment.   2. Marriage.   HQ 536 S582d]
  HQ536.S497   1992
  306.872—dc20
  DNLM/DLC
  for Library of Congress

Printed in the United States of America
10 9 8 7 6 5 4 3 2 1

for Michael, Emily, and Chelsey

Contents

Preface

Within the home and within society, dual-career marriage constitutes a system in transition. Each dual-career marriage is constantly in flux, as careers evolve, children grow, and marital relations change. And within modern society, the ways in which husbands and wives juggle two careers with family life continue to shift over time. At issue at both levels of transition—marital and sociohistorical—are changing gender roles. Dual-career marriage offers a revealing glimpse at the evolution of gender roles underway in contemporary society.

Of many narratives (e.g., political, economic, religious) that one could tell about contemporary Western society, one compelling story-line belongs to the marked shift in gender roles. The majority of men and women now in dual-career marriages grew up in families with a breadwinner father and a homemaker mother. Questions such: as "How will I fit work and family together?" "How will my spouse and I divide roles at home and in the world?" "Who will care for our children?" are relevant and pressing for men and women today in a way both new and significant.

The challenges posed by adding a wife's career into the family equation seem substantial at a pragmatic level alone: Without a "homemaker," how does the home get made? More subtle and complex are the psychological challenges: How do changes in gender roles occur? What are the benefits and costs? What are the effects of the many years of observing more traditional gender roles between parents? What are the implications of years of expecting, enacting in play and elaborating in fantasy, an "ideal" marriage predicated on a gender-based division of work and family?

In order to explore these questions, I have examined a small sample of dual-career marriages (20 couples) at close range. I have sought to scrutinize how the lives of these 40 men and women both challenge established traditions of gender and continue to replicate, either by design or default, those deeply entrenched traditions.

This book grew out of my doctoral dissertation in psychology at Yale University. I extend my deepest thanks to Faye Crosby, my primary advisor, for her wisdom, criticism, guidance, and seemingly limitless encouragement, extending not only throughout the dissertation process but also during its transformation into this book. Her facilitation of my work has so dramatically exceeded the requirements of her role that it is hard to describe it or adequately express my gratitude. I thank Jesse Geller, my second advisor, for sharing generously his impressive gifts for divergent thinking and clinical insight and for a broad, rewarding colleagueship. The other members of my committee—William Kessen, Donald Quinlan, and Mindy Rosenberg—were thoughtful and supportive readers, who helped me find my way down the unorthodox path of qualitative dissertation research.

I am grateful to two funding sources that provided support for the research. I received a Dissertation Grant Award from the Society for the Psychological Study of Social Issues and a Women's Studies Dissertation Award from the Woodrow Wilson Foundation.

Although they must remain anonymous, the forty women and men who found time in their busy lives to answer my questions, with patience and honesty, receive my great appreciation. In addition, the couples who served as pilot subjects were enormously helpful to me in the formative stages of my project.

I acknowledge gratefully the contributions of many others to this project: Donald Greif, for his skillful interviewing; Claire Sokoloff, for early help in imagining how such a project could assume shape and form; Shan Guisinger, for constructive input and broad-based encouragement; Emily Weir, for careful and helpful editorial comments; Lisa Pagliaro, for expert assistance in manuscript preparation. I am grateful to Judith Amsel at Lawrence Erlbaum Associates for her continuous support of the book. Also, in the spirit of this book, I express my appreciation and admiration of Donna Smythe, Taryn Villano, Ann Rivera, and Priscilla Rivera, who have enabled me to do my work with peace of mind and have shown me the complexity and subtlety of quality child care.

This book is about the interface of work and family. It feels noteworthy that during the time that I have been working on this project I have also been immersed in creating my own dual-career family. I have had the interesting opportunity to reflect on my findings both before and after having children. This research has never felt "purely academic" to me. I have tried to remain aware of my personal connection to my topic and to use my training as a clinical psychologist to examine possible "countertransference" issues that might interfere with my objectivity and cloud the study. I have been relieved that the study has continued to ring true as I have begun to accrue my own experiences with dual-career family life.

I thank my parents, Morton and Estelle Silberstein, for generous and loving support of my efforts in both work and family. My daughters, Emily and Chelsey, have enabled me to appreciate, as I could only before imagine, the wondrous and powerful family side of the work-family equation. Finally and most profoundly, to my husband, Michael Barrios, I feel inexpressibly grateful, for being an enabling colleague, comrade, and spouse, and for allowing me to know and to feel the vitality and joy possible in dual-career marriage.

And as I watch my young daughters play "house" (both the mommy and daddy go to work, both tend the baby dolls, and the babysitter occupies a prominent role), I wonder how the story of dual-career marriage will unfold in the generations to come.

Lisa R. Silberstein
New Haven, CT

Chapter 1

Dual-Career Marriage and the Worlds of Work and Family

Dual-career marriage, in which wife and husband each pursue a professional career, offers a window onto the changing landscape of gender roles and relations. In the span of a single generation, the family in which both parents work outside the home has gone from being the exception to being the rule. In 1985, both husband and wife worked in 64% of married couple families with children under 18, and half of the mothers with children under 3 were in the workforce, up from one third in 1975 (U.S. Department of Labor, 1985).

What implications does this impressive, rapid change hold for the fabric of family and marital life and for the course of men's and women's work lives? To what extent does the modern dual-career marriage challenge and rearrange traditional gender patterns, and to what extent does it replicate the essential gender arrangements of traditional marriage?

This volume aims to illuminate the multilayered issues involved in combining two careers and a family under one roof. The wives and husbands of 20 dual-career marriages with children were interviewed intensively about four major issues:

1. How are their dual-career marriages similar to and different from traditional one-career marriages?
2. How do the two careers develop side by side, and in what ways do dual-career spouses help or hinder each other's careers?
3. How do work and family combine in dual-career marriages?

1

4. How are relationships between spouses and between parents and children affected by the dual careers?

It is important to note that the majority of working women (and working men) work in *jobs* rather than *careers*. Careers are distinguished from jobs in that careers require a high degree of commitment, develop continuously (Rapoport & Rapoport, 1976), and typically require at least a bachelor's degree. However, increasing numbers of women are pursuing careers rather than jobs. For example, in 1970, women earned 7% of all medical degrees and 5% of all law degrees; in 1985, 28% of medical degrees and 37% of law degrees were awarded to women (U.S. Department of Education, 1985).

Of professional women who marry, the vast majority marry men who also have professional careers (Astin, 1969; Feldman, 1973). Thus, as the number of women pursuing professional careers continues to rise, the number of dual-career marriages can also be expected to increase. Before 1970, marriages in which the wife as well as the husband pursued careers were exceptional, even aberrant phenomena on the fringe of mainstream culture. A review of the popular press as well as scholarly literature suggests that today dual-career marriages occupy center stage in the drama of changing gender roles.

Research into dual-career marriages began in the late 1960s, yielding qualitative portraits of the dual-career *pioneers* (Rapoport & Rapoport, 1971). Since then, researchers have focused primarily on specific aspects of dual-worker or dual-career marriages. Given the dramatic changes that have occurred since the initial research on dual-career couples, it is striking that, other than unreliable reports in the popular press, a multidimensional portrait of contemporary dual-career couples is lacking.

Dual-career marriages occupy a small corner of the universe of dual-worker marriages and represent a highly privileged group. Hence, they cannot be seen as representative of all marriages in which both spouses are employed. However, women in dual-career marriages have entered the upper echelons of male employment and, hence, are making strides toward greater gender equality at work. As a result, their marriages comprise a fascinating and apt focus for studying change and stasis in the family and in the interface of the worlds of work and home.

In the current era of divorce, it must be recognized that this is a study of survivors. The stories of the casualties of dual-career marriages are likely to read differently and require their own investigation.

The current investigation of dual-career marriage grows out of and builds on previous research on how women and men engage in work and family life, how these areas interact, and how women's forays into the world of work have influenced the involvements of both genders in family and work. In briefly reviewing earlier studies, we first consider research on the worlds of work and family. Then, we turn to the effects of dual employment on marriage, on domestic life, and on husbands' and wives' careers. Finally, we examine the role of expectations in dual-worker marriage.

THE MYTH OF SEPARATE WORLDS

The dual-career marriage is, at its core, an attempt to redefine the relationship between work and family, the two primary spheres of modern life. The traditional marriage between husband and wife has been an interpersonal marriage between work and family: He worked outside of the home, and she worked inside it. In the dual-career marriage, each spouse combines the two spheres; the marriage of work and family is now intrapersonal as well as interpersonal.

The longstanding assignment of each gender to a single sphere contributed to a blindspot in scholarship on work and family. Researchers and theorists have been slow to recognize a relationship between the spheres of work and family. A *myth of separate worlds* has prevailed historically in research on work and family (Kanter, 1977). The family has been studied with insufficient attention to work, and research on work has largely ignored the influence of family.

A powerful influence behind the perceived separation of work and family has been the distinct association of each domain not only with a different gender but also with a different way of being. Work has been viewed as masculine and instrumental, whereas the family has been seen as feminine and expressive (Parsons & Bales, 1955).[1] Men's roles in both worlds have done little to shake the myth of separate worlds. In contrast, when women began to enter the paid workforce in significant numbers, the neat gender-linked division of work and family was challenged.

Researchers have only recently begun to approach work and family as interrelated phenomena. Attention has been directed increasingly toward men at home as well as at work and toward women at work as well as at home. As Bronfenbrenner and Crouter (1982) asserted, an understanding of one part of this system of work and family cannot be

---

[1]Stewart and Malley (1987) observed that both work and family roles contain both instrumental and expressive dimensions, and that further attention needs to be paid to these *within*-role characteristics.

achieved without attention to the functioning of other parts. Pleck (1977) defined the *work-family role system* as encompassing the male work role, female work role, male family role, and female family role.

The ways in which the cognitive and affective dimensions of one domain "spill over" into or influence the other domain have received initial exploration. Kanter (1977) stressed the importance of examining dimensions of work that affect family relations and characteristics of family life that influence work. Consistent with traditional gender roles, Pleck (1977) suggested that the work-family boundary is *asymmetrically permeable*, with women experiencing spillover from home into work and men having spillover from work into home. In a study of blue-collar and clerical workers, Crouter (1984) found that mothers reported more spillover of a negative, distracting nature than fathers and that women with young children were the most likely group of either gender to report high levels of spillover from home into work.

The present study explores how work and family are balanced by each spouse individually and by the couple collectively. The study also examines the extent and nature of crossover of the work-family boundary in dual-career husbands and wives.

Marriage and Dual Careers

Approximately a half century ago, the sociologist Talcott Parsons introduced an assumption into the literature that continues to be a source of inquiry and controversy. Parsons (1940, 1942) asserted that a woman's work involvement would necessarily be a source of marital strain, upsetting the unity of status that derives from only one family member (the husband) comprising the source of family status. He stressed the importance of keeping lines of achievement segregated and not directly comparable in order to avert jealousy and a sense of inferiority. Whereas men were expected to be the sole determinants of family status, women were assigned singular responsibility for the family's emotional welfare and children's development. The traditional dictum of family life could be summarized as, "A man owes to his profession what a woman owes to her family" (Coser & Rokoff, 1971).

Research on dual-worker marriage does not support Parsons' prediction that working wives would disrupt the solidarity of marriage. Wife employment does not affect significantly either wife's or husband's ratings of marital satisfaction (Staines, Pleck, Shepard, & O'Connor, 1978), unless she participates in the labor market out of economic necessity rather than by choice (Orden & Bradburn, 1963). Furthermore, little support has been found for Parsons' notion that marriage would be most endangered when a wife's occupational prestige equalled or surpassed her husband's (Philliber & Hiller, 1983; Richardson, 1979; Simpson & England, 1981).

Although dual-worker marriages in general do not show diminished satisfaction, dual-career marriages may encounter particular challenges. Women's pursuit of careers rather than jobs may introduce some complications into their marriages. Female professionals have higher divorce rates than either women in general or professional men (Centra, 1975; Epstein, 1973; Rosow & Rose, 1972). This suggests that, at least for some couples, dual-career status may be a factor in marital breakup. Advanced education for women may also be a risk factor for marital distress. Women with one year or more of graduate education have a higher rate of separation and divorce than women with college degrees; the rate of marital disruption in these women with postcollege education is exceeded only by women who do not finish high school (Houseknecht & Spanier, 1980). A large survey found that men of varying achievement orientations felt marriage to a relatively more educated wife to be stressful; achievement-oriented women experienced marriage to a comparatively more educated husband to be satisfying (Hornung & McCullough, 1981).

Perhaps women with high occupational attainments can afford to divorce more than women with less well-paying employment. Macroeconomic analyses support the idea that women who can support themselves and any children are more likely to leave an unhappy marriage (Ross & Sawhill, 1975). However, the wives' high income also appears to contribute to marital distress. Yankelovich (1974) observed that many men experience their work as worthwhile because it provides for family needs and that working wives undermine this source of male identity and pride. Garland (1972) found in a study of 53 dual-career couples that the single factor having a negative effect on the quality of married life was the wife having a higher income than the husband. Similarly, Hardesty and Betz (1980) found that although higher family income was associated with increased marital satisfaction for both spouses in dual-career marriages, the higher the wife's income, the less satisfying the marriage. These data suggest some validity to Parsons' hypothesis that dismantling the man's role as provider and as primary source of family status destabilizes marriage.

In light of this evidence that the wives' career attainments may pose a challenge to marriage, a question arises how the early dual-career couples experienced the pursuit of careers by both wives and husbands. Two not wholly compatible observations are salient (Rice, 1979). First, the dual-career couples recognized that they were engaged in a highly stressful lifestyle (Bebbington, 1973; Burke & Weir, 1976; Holmstrom, 1972; Johnson & Johnson, 1977; Rapoport & Rapoport, 1969; St. John-Parsons, 1978). The dual-career couples depicted considerable stresses associated with the practical aspects of juggling two careers and a family. Role strain was considered a central issue in the life of the dual-career wife (Bebbington, 1973; Heckman, Bryson, & Bryson, 1977; Holmstrom, 1972; Johnson & Johnson, 1977; Rapoport & Rapoport, 1971).[2] At another level, the couples described issues involved in going against societal norms and expectations and in developing a lifestyle without role models (Bebbington, 1973; Holmstrom, 1972; Rapoport & Rapoport, 1971).

Second, and strikingly, these early dual-career couples did not attribute their stress to issues of comparison and competition, as Parsons had predicted. Instead, the couples exhibited a pronounced tendency to deny marital conflict, especially stemming from feelings of competition. Rice (1979) suggested that the dual-career couples' denial of conflict may have resulted from two sources: a need to reduce cognitive dissonance arising from the conflicting demands of work and family and a desire to avoid confronting apparent inequities in the relationship.

Relevant to consideration of these potential strains—work-family conflicts and inequities in the relationship—was a consistent pattern in the early dual-career couples of the wives' careers remaining secondary to the husbands'. The wives often left the workforce during the early child-rearing years. Wives also devoted less time to their careers and more time to home and family than did their husbands. This alleviated some role strain problems (Johnson & Johnson, 1976). In addition, husbands' careers maintained primary status in the family in the eyes of both the wife and husband, avoiding the symmetrical marriage that was viewed as potentially debilitating. The tendency of women to "put a lid" on their aspirations (Rossi, 1965) may have prevented competitive anxieties from being roused in their husbands and themselves (Poloma & Garland, 1971).

By compromising their career ambitions, these dual-career wives, studied in the late 1960s and early 1970s, thus circumvented some of the dilemmas that were hypothesized to be troublesome aspects of dual-career marriage. Do today's dual-career wives devise and accept similar solutions? A survey of professional married women in the early

---

[2]Role theory has been invoked to hypothesize about and describe working women's role strain, defined as "the felt difficulty in fulfilling role obligations" (Goode, 1960). Other concepts that have been applied to working women are role overload (the feeling that role obligations add up to being too much to do) and role conflict (the feeling that obligations of multiple roles pull the person in different directions). Unfortunately, use of these terms has been inconsistent in the literature, and rarely have the concepts been operationalized in standard or similar ways across studies.

1980s suggests that they may be less likely than women surveyed a decade earlier to limit their professional involvement (Gray, 1983). This volume examines the extent to which contemporary dual-career wives accommodate their careers for family and/or for their husbands' careers and the effects of these actions for women, men, and their marriages.

Domestic Careers

From a work-family systems perspective, the question arises whether women's foray into the male occupational world has precipitated a reciprocal increase in men's participation in the female domestic world. It was predicted that dual-career couples represented a movement toward increased symmetry of both work and family roles for men and women (Young & Willmott, 1973). Because dual-career wives were breaking gender-role barriers in the workplace, they were expected to lead the way toward equity at home as well.

In general, research on dual-worker couples shows a minimal impact of wife employment on husband involvement in domestic tasks (Berk & Berk, 1979; Meissner, Humphreys, Meis, & Scheu, 1975; Nickols & Metzen, 1978; Walker & Woods, 1976). As Hochschild (1989) described, women's daytime paid employment (the first shift) resulted in strikingly small changes in their responsibilities for the second shift at home. However, dual-career couples may be more likely than other dual-worker couples to share domestic work (Hochschild, 1989). Some research suggests that husbands contribute more to family work if their wives earn more (Barnett, 1983; Gilbert, 1985; Haas, 1982a; Model, 1982; Ross, Mirowsky, & Huber, 1983; Scanzoni, 1979). In contrast, other researchers found that although a wife's education level affected her husband's participation in the home, her income level had no effect (Eriksen, Yancy, & Eriksen, 1979; Farkas, 1976).

A related dimension that has been hypothesized to affect husband involvement in domestic work is the degree of the wife's psychological investment in her job. Bahr (1974) observed that high work-committed women received less help from their husbands than low work-committed women, perhaps because husbands felt more constrained to help around the house if the wives were working to meet a financial need of the family. In contrast, more recent research suggests that when a husband perceives his wife as highly committed to her work, he is more likely to participate in domestic work (Gilbert, 1985).

If dual-career husbands are increasing their participation in family work, which aspects of the family role are men most likely to adopt? Weingarten (1978) found that dual-career spouses equitably divided household tasks other than child care. Weingarten suggested that this reflects the closer association of child care with the feminine role and men's sense that child-care duties therefore threaten their masculinity. In contrast, Gilbert (1985) found that a greater proportion of dual-career husbands assumed child-care tasks than household responsibilities, perhaps reflecting the greater rewards inherent to child care than housework.

It is unclear to what extent inequity of domestic labor troubles couples. Yogev (1981), for example, found that although professional women devoted almost three times as many hours per week to housework and child care as their husbands, a very small minority of women believed that their husbands were not doing an appropriate share. Women's discontent with low spousal involvement in domestic chores may be higher in dual-career couples than other dual-worker couples. For example, one study found that women college graduates showed a steeper increase between 1966 and 1973 than less educated women in their desire to have husbands help with household chores (Robinson, 1977). This volume considers for whom the inequitable division of domestic labor becomes problematic and what then happens.

A number of questions therefore remain about how dual-career couples divide domestic work, which the current research addresses. To what extent has the traditional division of chores shifted to a more equal distribution of responsibilities? How does a new approach to division of domestic work evolve? How is the new approach experienced by men, who are adopting roles previously ascribed to females, and by women, who are sharing responsibilities that were formerly under sole female jurisdiction?

Two Careers Under One Roof

The dual-career marriage distinguishes itself from the traditional marriage by the wife's pursuit of a career. Are the career pursuits of husband and wife comparable? How does the concurrent development of two careers in a marriage influence each career?

As observed above, in early dual-career couples, the wives tended to accommodate their careers both to their husbands' careers and to their children. Poloma and Garland (1971) concluded that women's *tolerance of domestication* represents a major obstacle to married women's realization of their full occupational potential. Some survey research supports a view that family life may represent an impediment to career success for women. Although marriage is associated with greater success for men compared to remaining single, women who marry achieve less occupational success than women who remain single

(Feldman, 1973; Havens, 1973; Mueller & Campbell, 1977). Coser and Rokoff (1971), for example, found that among women with doctorate degrees, those who remained single were far more likely to attain associate or full professor rank than married women. In contrast, another study found that marriage and motherhood did not affect publication rates of women scientists (Cole & Zuckerman, 1987). It has also been suggested that marriage can be an asset to a woman's career. Epstein (1987) reported that the most successful female lawyers are married; perhaps this is related to married women's greater access to male networks compared to their single counterparts (Kaufman, 1978). Further research is needed to determine the factors associated with how much women will compromise their career ambitions to accommodate their husbands' careers and family demands.

Geographic mobility is an important way women may accommodate their own careers to their husbands. Wallston, Foster, and Berger (1978) reported that when dual-career couples are presented with hypothetical vignettes about job-seeking, they describe egalitarian decision-making rules. However, a consistent pattern of results suggests that the wives' job opportunities have carried considerably less weight than their husbands' in determining the couple's geographic location (Duncan & Perucci, 1976; Ferber & Huber, 1979; Gilbert, 1985; Heckman, Bryson, & Bryson, 1977; Holmstrom, 1972; Poloma, Pendleton, & Garland, 1982). The wives' incomes appear to bear no influences on this pattern (Duncan & Perucci, 1976). These studies indicate that women are unlikely to relocate for their own careers but are likely to disrupt their careers in order for their husbands to relocate.

Research to date thus suggests that dual-career wives adapt their career paths to accommodate both family and husbands' careers. Questions that are addressed in this book include the extent to which this pattern of accommodation still pertains to today's dual-career couples. How do women and men experience this pattern? What do they think motivates it? Do women feel that they de-escalate their career ambitions (Epstein, 1986) by choice or out of necessity?

How does dual-career marriage affect men's careers? If the wife is no longer fulfilling the role of full-time nurturer and home manager, what is the effect on the husband's ability to perform in the occupational world? Professional men often relied on their wives to provide professional back-up (e.g., as unpaid research assistants and secretaries) and social supports (e.g., as hostesses for business gatherings), a phenomenon that gave rise to the label of the *two-person career* (Papanek, 1973).

Based on a review of the literature on the relationship of spouse's education to career success in academia, Ferber and Huber (1979) wondered whether a new hierarchy among workers may emerge, with men married to less educated wives at the top, single men and women in the middle, and men and women with highly educated spouses at the bottom. The authors found, for example, that compared to husbands whose wives had less than a college education, husbands married to wives with a college education had published significantly fewer articles and held fewer offices. Consistent with this view, Osherson and Dill (1983) found that men in one-career marriages reported feeling more successful in their work than men in dual-career marriages. Interestingly, however, fathers in dual-career marriages felt more self-actualized at work than fathers in one-career marriages. The authors suggested that the one-career father may define success in more traditional terms as the provider, whereas shared family responsibilities and two paychecks increase the importance of self-development at work for dual-career fathers.

It is unclear from the literature the extent to which men in dual-career marriages today still wish to fulfill the traditional provider role and whether they view their dual-career marriages as impeding their career success.[3] Does the husband's career suffer when, instead of having a corporate wife, the wife has her own corporation? If dual-career husbands are carrying increased responsibility for domestic work, what effect does that have on their careers? These issues are also addressed in this volume.

The interrelationships between husbands' and wives' careers have received minimal attention, probably as an outgrowth of the historical perspective on the separation of work and family. To understand fully the dual-career marriage, both husband and wife must be studied as both subject and object. That is, one must examine the woman's relationship to her career, his career, and the marriage and the man's relationship to his career, her career, and the marriage. Typically,

---

[3]Although little research has examined the effects of a wife's employment on her husband's career, some research suggests that wife employment is associated with husbands' increased psychological distress (Burke & Weir, 1976; Kessler & McRae, 1982; Rosenfield, 1980). This is in contrast to the general finding that wives who work outside the home experience better mental health than their nonemployed counterparts (Baruch, Barnett, & Rivers, 1983; Crosby, 1982; Gove & Geerken, 1977). The negative impact of wife employment on husbands' well-being has been explained in terms of task demands and identity issues arising from the working wife's expectation that her husband participate in domestic work (Burke & Weir, 1976; Safilios-Rothschild & Dijkers, 1978). However, husbands' psychological distress does not seem to be associated with doing more housework (Ross et al., 1983) or child care (Kessler & McRae, 1982). It has been suggested, therefore, that gender-role orientations rather than objective workloads are implicated in men's responses to their wives' employment and that increased performance of domestic work may reflect greater comfort with wife employment.

studies of dual-earner and dual-career couples focus on the woman's relationship to her own career and the man's relationship to his wife's career but largely disregard the other factors in this matrix.

The Role of Expectations in Dual-Career Marriage

Although survey research suggests the importance of expectations in dual-worker marriage, qualitative research on dual-career marriage has not yet fully considered the role of expectations. As Kelley (1979) noted, marital interactions occur in a context of thought; each partner is guided by cognitions about the self and partner as well as about the interaction process. Three kinds of situations involving expectations are potential sources of conflict in the dual-worker marriage. First, a discrepancy between a person's expectations and his or her reality causes intrapersonal distress. For example, when mothers prefer not to work outside the home but are employed, psychological well-being suffers (Gove & Zeiss, 1987; Ross et al., 1983). Second, a lack of convergence between the expectations of the two spouses creates interpersonal tension. For example, when spouses differ about wife employment, marital satisfaction decreases (Pearlin, 1975). Finally, a mismatch between one's expectations and society's expectations creates problems. For instance, couples in which the wife is dominant show high marital dissatisfaction, perhaps because male dominance is the societal norm (Gray-Little & Burks, 1983).

In an era of transition, configurations of expectations about gender roles might be assumed to be complex and changing. How do gender roles evolve within the context of a marriage, and what are the implications of such changes? Lewis and Spanier (1979) concluded from their review of the marital satisfaction literature that marital quality is more related to the *congruence* of role expectations of one spouse and the role performance of the other than to a specific pattern of roles. Bowen and Orthner (1983) found that marital quality was lower in couples with "a traditional husband and modern wife" than in couples with congruent gender-role attitudes. Nettles and Loevinger (1983) reported greater differences in gender-role attitudes and behaviors between spouses in problem marriages (in either a phase of separation or counseling) than in nonproblem marriages.

Expectations are dynamic in two senses: historical and developmental. Some of the inconsistent results in the literature on the effects of female employment on individual well-being and marital satisfaction may relate to sociohistorical cohort differences (Kessler & McRae, 1981). Gender-role norms are evolving, and these societal level changes deserve further attention in psychological research. As Ste-

wart (1987) noted, psychologists have largely ignored research participants' experience of social history.

Changes in expectations also occur at the individual level. Rapoport
and Rapoport (1975) defined *identity tension lines* as the degree to
which each dual-career spouse can transcend earlier social condi-
tioning to take on tasks previously associated with the opposite gender. Tension is caused not only by performing out-of-role behavior but
also by *not* performing in-role behavior. The issues involved in
changing gender-role expectations related to work and family must be
considered within the systems context of both husband and wife.

How do once-traditional expectations and behaviors evolve into
more nontraditional gender perceptions and patterns? Hertz (1986)
concluded from a study of dual-career couples in business that they
often moved into more egalitarian behavior as a result of the workload
demands inherent to their two careers. However, evidence also suggests that change may occur in the reverse direction: Changing expectations may lead the way for changes in behavior. The women's
movement played a crucial role in a sample of Swedish couples'
decisions to share roles in their marriages (Haas, 1982a, 1982b) and in
a sample of American women's decisions to work continuously outside
of the home (Stewart, 1987). Researchers generally found that husband
participation in family tasks was influenced more by expectations
about gender roles and an ideological commitment to parity in the
home than by a large burden of child care (Baruch & Barnett, 1981) or
by men's time availability (Bohen & Viveros-Long, 1981; Perucci,
Potter, & Rhoads, 1978).

The evidence thus suggests that at least some change in expectations must occur for nontraditional behaviors (e.g., role sharing) to
evolve. The processes by which and the degrees to which behavior in
the dual-career marriage shapes expectations and expectations shape
behavior deserve further attention. When one spouse's expectations
change about the division of work and family roles, the effects on the
individual, the partner, and the marriage are likely to be unsettling.
Research needs to examine how spouses cope with such tensions and
how expectations evolve within the individual and within the marriage.

A WINDOW ONTO GENDER ROLES IN TRANSITION

Contemporary dual-career couples provide a window onto gender roles
in transition. On the one hand, the dual-career family is emerging as a
normative family arrangement within certain strata of society. On the
other hand, dual-career spouses were raised with traditional assump-

tions of male breadwinner and female homemaker roles. Furthermore, despite the increasing norm of employment for mothers, the traditional assumptions of male breadwinner and female homemaker continue to enshroud government policies, employment practices, and much of society's attitudes (Hoffman, 1985).

Very little attention has been directed to the ways in which dual-career spouses perceive continuities and discontinuities between their own lives and those of their parents. Strikingly little research has examined how men and women negotiate these marked intergenerational shifts, intrapersonally and interpersonally. Examination of this issue offers a rich opportunity to consider the nature of change between generations and the complexities inherent to evolving gender roles.

In summary, dual-career spouses might be expected to contain not only consciously altered expectations (about gender roles, work, family, and marriage) but also deeply socialized, internalized, and probably change-resistant experiences, emotional needs, and entrenched patterns of behavior. To what extent are the anticipated changes toward increased symmetry at work and at home occuring, and to what extent are traditional patterns persisting? An examination is needed not only of the conflicts engendered by change but also of the multitude of ways in which people cope with transition.

Changes in women's involvement in occupational work and men's involvement in domestic work have occurred within a strikingly brief span of time. It would be predicted that men and women may carry different expectations about work and family into their marriages than individuals who differ in age by as little as 10 years. The current research project focuses on a specific age group: young dual-career couples with children. At the same time, the study seeks to explore the ways in which sociocultural cohort differences affect expectations about and patterns of dual-career family life. The designated sample is, therefore, women and men born between 1943 and 1953, who were aged 32 to 42 at the time of participation in the study.

Competing hypotheses can be posed about the challenges facing these younger and older dual-career couples today. On the one hand, younger couples have experienced the societal changes regarding gender roles at an earlier age and thus might be more likely to enter marriage expecting that both spouses will maintain full commitment to professional careers. Older couples, who have evolved a dual-career lifestyle but did not necessarily grow up or enter marriage anticipating it, may experience relatively more conflict between their internalized expectations for marriage, family, and work and their present reality.

On the other hand, *because* of their socialization experiences and original expectations for a marriage with man as primary breadwinner, these older couples may be more likely than their younger counterparts to preserve the salience of the work sphere for husbands and the domestic sphere for wives. Hence, the older couples might be likely to resolve potential tensions (e.g., role strain and competition) in similar ways to earlier dual-career couples. Compared to older dual-career wives, younger women in the sample may be less likely to accommodate or compromise their careers for husband's career or for family, hence placing the younger couples into a situation of potentially heightened conflict at both pragmatic and psychological levels.[4]

AN OVERVIEW OF THE RESEARCH

Answers to the kinds of questions to be examined in this volume emerge from personal accounts that probe the corners and crevices of people's intimate lives. These corners remain largely inaccesible to research by questionnaire. An intensive interview enables close and detailed exploration of both subjective and objective levels of people's lives. Richly textured descriptions provide a vantage point from which to examine cultural themes and their impact on individual psychologies. As Rapoport and Rapaport (1976) contended, the researcher operating in this anthropological way approaches the couple not only as a specimen of its society and culture, but also as a lens to provide insight into crucial psychological and social processes.

This volume is based on extensive interviews with 20 married couples between the ages of 32 and 42. (For a detailed description of the research method, see Appendix A.) Each participant had an active, professional career, and each couple had at least one child from the current marriage. Nearly three quarters of the participants had advanced degrees, and their average household income was $94,000.

Each spouse was interviewed individually for two sessions lasting up to 2 hours each. The interview questions are listed in Appendix B. Responses to the questions were categorized and form the basis for the chapters that follow. Where useful, percentages of responses in each category are presented. However, given the nature of small sample, qualitative research, general trends are often more important to examine than specific numbers. The following terms are used when presenting trends: *a few* (15%-25%), *a third* or *many* (30%-40%), *half*

---

[4]Nadelson and Eisenberg (1977) suggested, for example, that the challenge to the husband's narcissism will be greater when *co-equal sacrifice* is demanded at the beginning of marriage than when a husband already well established in his career encourages his wife to begin or accelerate her own career.

(45%-55%), a majority (60%-75%), and almost all (80% or more). In order to capture the flavor of the responses, direct quotations from the participants are frequently presented. Unless otherwise specified, a direct quotation is representative of responses in its category.

Four main categories of issues form the core of the research and comprise the content of the next four chapters. Chapter 2 explores the sources of continuity and change between the current dual-career marriages and the traditional marriages of earlier generations. We explore if gender-linked expectations remain true: Is work still more salient for men than women, and is family more salient for women than men? This pair of expectations forms the legacy of contemporary marriage, either to be embraced or challenged by the dual-career couples. Chapter 3 moves to an examination of issues involved in two careers developing side by side: the career paths of husbands and wives, the ways in which spouses facilitate and impede each other's careers, and issues of comparison and competition. We then consider, in chapter 4, the work and family system: the effect of family on careers, the ways in which work and family fit together in dual-career marriage, and the evolution of roles within the marriage.

In chapter 5, we focus on how dual careers have affected the heart of family life: children and marital intimacy. Finally, in chapter 6, we consider the implications of the findings for understanding dual-career marriage as a system in transition. The current sample is compared to earlier dual-career couples to highlight points of both stasis and change.

As Rose (1984) observed in her study of Victorian couples, marriage represents in microcosm the management of power between men and women. Marriage is, asserted John Stuart Mill, the primary political experience in which most of us engage as adults. Jacoby (1975) observed, "The social does not 'influence' the private; it dwells within it" (p. 104). This study of dual-career couples offers a lens onto the simultaneously personal and political arrangements of gender in marriage and onto the changing interrelationship between the worlds of work and family.

Chapter 2

Gender, Work, and Family: Continuity and Change

It's not like I made a conscious decision that I was going to be a professional woman and not do what women of my mother's generation did. I just always assumed that I would go to college and pursue my interests. In many ways, the transition was absolutely abrupt—it ended with my mother, and then I felt encouraged to go after a career. It's kind of an amazing transition, now that I think of it. It hasn't really sunk in before. How remarkable it is that things have changed so fast.

—A lawyer in her upper-30s

I remember my sister saying to my mother, "Gee, sometimes it seems like Dad is a guest in our house." I doubt my children would ever say that about me. My father—we didn't have an intimate association with him. And he didn't have as full a sense of us, from day-to-day dealing with us. I could have this relationship with my kids without being part of a dual-career couple. But because I am part of one, I don't have any choice, and I think I do better when I don't have a choice. And sometimes the more difficult things are the most satisfying.

—An architect in his early 40s

I don't know why I don't hold all those stereotypes, that mothers should stay home with the kids. I grew up in a very traditional, lower middle-class family, and all the mothers I knew stayed home. So I should have all those stereotypes. It's exactly the right place to get them all!

—A scientist in her early 40s

16

A dual-career family structure represents a significant and profound departure from the families within which the women and men in the study grew up. The majority of the dual-career spouses grew up in one-career families, in which their fathers were breadwinners and their mothers were homemakers.

Two thirds of the participants' mothers were full-time housewives during the participants' childhood. The other one third of the mothers worked at least part time or intermittently during the participants' childhood. Only a few mothers worked full time. Several of the employed mothers were single parents, and a few worked in family-based businesses (e.g., farming, family stores). None of the participants' mothers had a career of comparable level to the women in the dual-career sample.

What implications does such intergenerational change carry for individuals and couples? How do the men and women in the study experience and understand the differences between the gender arrangements of their childhood families and their current families? Where and to what extent do they see continuities and discontinuities between the lives of their parents and their own lives?

Families of origin provide early models of gender roles that often determine expectations and templates for later experience. How have these expectations changed over time? What happens to these early encoded models in the wake of a sociocultural redefinition of marriage and family life?

INTERGENERATIONAL CHANGE

Let us turn first to one source of many expectations: one's parents. Participants reported that their parents served as both positive and negative role models regarding work and family. The relationships of the dual-career spouses' lives to their parents' are described in three categories: doing what their parents did, doing what their parents did *not* do, and *not* doing what their parents *did* do.

Doing What Parents Did

The fact that the dual-career spouses have created work and family roles that differ in important respects from their parents does not undermine many powerful influences of their parents on their lives. The majority of participants reported incorporating core values of the traditional roles from their same-sex parents: mothering for women, employment for men. A woman in her upper-30s, whose mother did not work outside the home, spoke of how she strove to carry on aspects of her mother's parenting style: "My mother was a nurturer, and devoted a lot of her life to helping us enjoy the world in a creative way—reading to us, playing games, pointing out things. I've incorporated that." Many women mentioned particular aspects of their mother's role that they sought to preserve, such as holiday baking or faithful attendance at school functions, despite the time challenges they pose to a working mother. An executive in her late 30s remarked:

> It's interesting. There's a funny pull in me about my obligations as a mother, an enormous pull about the things a woman does to keep her house and family together. I guess they're all old-fashioned kinds of things that I picked up from my mother, my grandmother. I've just naturally rearranged my schedule to fit it all in.

Although women's careers appear more different from than similar to their mothers' lives, one third of the women felt that their mothers provided some positive modeling for their work lives. Women whose mothers worked outside the home or were active in volunteer or community activities spoke of internalizing what one woman called a *do-orientation* from their mothers. More explicit than most was the view of one woman in her mid-30s that her mother, who worked full time, had been a role model in her own career development: "Since my dad died when I was young, my mother brought us up as a single parent. So even though we've never talked about it, I think she was a role model— a woman who worked, was self-sufficient."

People bring to marriage expectations not only about their own roles but also about the roles of their spouses. For example, many women expected that their husbands should be successful men like their fathers. This assumption was derived not only from their fathers but also from their mothers, who held similar expectations of marrying a successful man. One third of the men talked about feeling an expectation from their wives to resemble the wives' fathers in terms of work success. A man in government in his mid-30s stated:

> I think she's more invested in my career being successful than I am in hers. She is a child of a doctor who was often out to work and at conferences at night, and so that's fine with her if I work hard and at night. She would get worried if I stopped doing that. She expects to be married to a successful man, like her father.

Infrequently, these expectations worked in the opposite direction. A highly ambitious man in his mid-30s felt that his father-in-law's comparatively less ambitious career has contributed to his wife's view that he works too much: "Her father was a moderately successful man, with a satisfying if not outstanding career and a happy family life. So I don't think she sees why I feel driven to go beyond moderate success."

Men's expectations for themselves mirrored women's expectations for their husbands to be successful. For the majority of men, the key aspect of their fathers' lives that they sought to continue was work devotion and success:

> When I think about it, my life looks a lot like my father's in a major way, despite all the changes: I put a lot of my energies into my work, and so did he. He used to be the only one in the family like that, since my mother didn't work, whereas now my wife is into her job too. But I know a lot of my drive to be successful comes from my father.

The dual-career spouses thus perceived the major continuities between their parents' lives and their own lives in terms of work for men and family for women. Next we see that the intergenerational discontinuities pertain to men's involvement at home and women's involvement at work.

Doing What Parents Did *Not* Do

Almost all of the women in the sample spoke of their careers as distinguishing them from their mothers. A range of feelings accompanied this recognition. For many women, their achievements represent some vindication of their mothers' frustrated aspirations. An architect in her early 40s stated: "My sister and I used to feel angry for her and with her, because back then, once you were married, women were not allowed to work with her firm anymore." A professor in her mid-30s commented: "I think most of the motivation for my career came from my mother, at least partly because of her frustration at her inability to fulfill her career aspirations." Many dual-career wives experienced their mothers as living vicariously through them and their achievements. An administrator in her mid-30s stated: "I think my mother has been delighted and is very proud of my career. At this point, her discontent with her life is assessed by comparison with me, and she has a need to live vicariously through me, because she sees I am a satisfied person."

Many women perceived their mothers as having been depressed, frustrated, and bored with their lives. They viewed their mothers' lives as characterized by limited and unsatisfying sources of gratification. A lawyer in her mid-30s commented:

> When I think about my mother, I picture this lovely, intelligent, charming woman, who was really very depressed all the time. I picture her standing at the ironing board, ironing handkerchiefs and pillowcases. I consider myself very fortunate: I go out to an exciting job every day, and I never iron.

An academic in her early 40s stated: "I look at my mother, and realize she was bored, because she did so little in life. She didn't know she was bored, she just nagged my father." An artist in her upper-30s remarked: "My mother is bitter that she only had roles as wife and mother. She would have loved to do something different. And she's resentful." An administrator in her upper-30s queried: "Are there people like that anymore—who are dependent on someone else for a definition of themselves? It sounds awful." Several women explicitly aimed to avoid what they perceived to be pitfalls in their mothers' lives. A businesswoman in her late 30s saw her mother as having devoted herself entirely to husband and children. When left without them, she found herself purposeless:

> When my father died, my mother was 50. She had nothing to do until she died. I don't see myself falling apart at age 50, with the kids in college, if I were widowed or divorced. I'd still have a structure to my life. That's really important to me.

Most women empathized with their mothers' situations, and said that they felt fortunate to have been born female a generation later rather than a generation sooner.

A few women viewed their career orientation as directly derived from their mothers. Meg, a professor in her early 40s, commented:

> My mother—I wouldn't want to sell her short. She gave a lot of encouragement for what she couldn't do but wanted her daughters to do. She tells me now that she was consciously pushing me all along.

However, about half the women attributed their career drive to their fathers. Meg remarked elsewhere: "My father is a pusher. The majority of my drive and ambition comes from him." A physician in her late 30s proclaimed: "My father was so into my career that he was worried when I got married and then when I had kids that I would give up my career." In this transitional generation, when female gender roles are expanding to include the traditional bastions of male roles, cross-gender parental influence (i.e., father-daughter) appears to be an important contribution to the nontraditional (i.e., work) roles.

Whereas women viewed their careers as differentiating them from their mothers, men felt that their greater involvement with children and home distinguished them from their fathers. A man in his mid-30s commented:

> My father had very little to do with household chores or childrearing. Jane and I aren't quite equal, but we approach it. This change has been all for the better— it's a sense of equality in home and in work. It's one of the most profound changes that has occurred in my lifetime.

Many men spoke of a desire to correct perceived deficiencies in the fathering that they had received. A man in his upper-30s declared:

> I relish the chance to bring up a kid the way I wish I had been brought up. Experience may prove a fool of me, but I have a real sense of wanting to give my son quality and quantity of attention. And I think that my instincts are right. I want to be more involved, more supportive in his upbringing than I feel my father was in mine.

Among the parents of the dual-career spouses, wife employment seemed to have had no effect on husband involvement in parenting and home care. Therefore, men who grew up with working mothers reported a dramatic change between their fathers' participation in the dual-worker home and their own involvement. A man in his early 30s whose mother worked full time said:

> My mother clearly had two jobs: working and the kids and household. My father just worked. I have much more involvement in the household and kids. If I think about it, I feel angry about my father not having participated more in my upbringing. But I learned from it.

Men's anger and resentment toward their fathers was a frequent theme (appearing explicitly and spontaneously in over one third of the men's interviews). Men generally respected their fathers' work success but felt deprived of the fathers' attention and interest. This memory of a work-preoccupied and emotionally removed father may temper high achievement motivation in the dual-career husband, as one man in his mid-30s explained:

> I remember my father struggling with his career, feeling he needed to devote all his time to it. And he discouraged me from staying in Boy Scouts, because he felt he would need to participate and he didn't want to give the time. Without his support, I discontinued. I haven't really thought of it before, but I think that was probably a counteracting force

against my careerist tendencies. I want to spend time with my children, and be available in a way that my father wasn't.

This father-son theme is quite different from the mother-daughter relationship that was primarily characterized by the daughter's empathy for the limitations of her mother's life. Few women felt deprived of something from their mothers in the way that men felt deprived of their fathers' attention. Although both men and women in the dual-career marriage are engaged in redefinitions of their same-gender parental roles, the directions of these shifts are polar opposites.

Women rarely articulated anger or resentment about their fathers' lack of involvement in the family in the ways and to the extent that men did. Perhaps this reflects something essential about relationships with the same-gender parent or the unique qualities of the father-son dyad. At the same time, however, many of the women are now committed to having their husbands highly involved with family and child care. Beyond the pragmatic and ideological reasons for this shared responsibility, it seems plausible that it may originate in the women's own experience of absent fathers. A woman in her mid-30s described this directly:

> I remember very little of my dad during my childhood. Sure, the big events—family trips, special occasions—but not the day-to-day stuff. Did he ever read me a story at bedtime? I don't know. Our children will have a very different experience of Calvin being there for them, and that's really important.

Although virtually all the men felt that they were involved with their children more than their fathers, it is clear that this increased involvement is relative. A man in his late 30s, whose wife carries the vast majority of child-care responsibilities (by both their accounts), stated: "I have a very different involvement with the kids than my father. I'll talk to the kids on the phone during the day, and scold them—or at night discipline them for how they treated their mother earlier." In contrast to the increased involvement at home, a few men commented on having less time for family due to more demanding and time-consuming careers than their fathers. (One third of the fathers of the dual-career spouses worked at jobs rather than careers.) A professor in his mid-30s stated:

> My father didn't have a career that required him to bring work home, or put the same kind of demands on him. My parents spent a tremendous amount of time with us, and I don't expect that I'll spend as much time with my child. And I don't honestly believe that quality can make up for quantity.

Related to but also distinct from child-care responsibilities are household chores. The majority of men felt that they contributed to the running of the household considerably more than had their fathers. A businessman in his mid-30s noted:

> It's interesting. I emulate my father in terms of career, but I'm totally different in things around the house. He was totally incompetent at all that. Well, actually, I always thought there were things he *could* do, but just didn't.

A man in his early 40s, whose parents ran a family business, said:

> I'm sure my father would be appalled to sit around and watch all that I do at home. He worked all day long beside my mother, and then she'd do all the cooking and cleaning, while he'd retire in the corner and recover for dinner.

Household chores, as one might expect, tended to be viewed as less rewarding than child care. However, men made some positive attributions for their increased household role. A man in his upper-30s proclaimed: "I find it almost liberating doing all this work around the house. I've discovered all sorts of interests, like cooking."

Some men attributed to their mothers their openness and ability to take on the traditionally female tasks of child care and housework. Perhaps this is analogous to the cross-gender parental influence in women who felt that their career motivation came from their fathers. A man in his early 40s stated:

> I think my mother was a major influence on my increased role in our home now. She believed that household tasks were not associated with gender—so I learned how to sew buttons on and iron. Of course, I fought it all the way as a kid, but I emerged as an adult who felt it important to be co-equal around the house.

A man in his upper-30s commented: "My mother was certainly no woman's libber, but she did influence me into believing what's fair is fair, and that a woman isn't the only one who should push a vacuum cleaner around."

The major differences between the lives of the dual-career spouses and their parents thus take the form of adopting roles of the cross-gender parent: employment for women and domestic tasks for men. In this transitional generation, there is some evidence that cross-gender parents may play a salient role. However, the dual-career spouses

experienced these changes more prominently in terms of discontinuities wih the same-gender parent rather than as continuities with the
cross-gender parent.

Not Doing What Parents *Did* Do

In counterpoint to doing what one's parents did not do (career for
women, home involvement for men), there is *not* doing that which
one's parents *did* do. For women, this consistently took two forms:
decreased time with children and decreased time and attention to the
household.

As is considered more extensively later, the issue of decreased time
with children occupies center stage in the world of many employed
mothers. Interestingly, few women directly compared themselves to
their own mothers on this dimension. This is in contrast to their
extensive discussions of their having careers compared to their
mothers not working outside the home. Perhaps the issue of child care
relative to their mothers is more emotionally charged and therefore
harder to talk about. Perhaps the comparison is so obvious that it tends
to go unmentioned, even unnoticed. Or perhaps when women express
concerns, thoughts, and feelings about spending time with their own
children, there is an unspoken, implicit message about the mothering
that they themselves received. It is as if a woman's own mother
represents the point of comparison implied in a statement that she is
spending less time with her children. It is as if the probing question,
"Am I spending enough time with my child?" has a second, silent
clause, "given that it is so much less time than my mother spent with
me?" A woman in her upper-30s commented:

> I suppose it may be a source of guilt that my mother was a full-time
> mother and I'm not. That's funny, though, because I've never thought
> about it. And believe me, I've thought a lot about this issue!

In addition to issues of child care, many women grapple with what it
means to have a different relationship to the home than their mothers
had. For their mothers, the home was a significant achievement
domain, often ranking second only to children. The home was something to work at and work for, and it yielded very concrete results.[5]

---

[5] Television advertisements both reflect and help create and amplify women's investment in the home as an achievement domain. In an analysis of over 500 television
commercials, Mamay and Simpson (1981) found that women were represented in only
three roles: maternal, housekeeping, and decorative. Women were depicted as endlessly
devoted in their attempts to please husband and children and in need of expert advice to
perfect their performance in these roles.

Women with careers may feel less attentive to their homes as show-cases because their achievement motivations are being funnelled into the workplace in addition to or instead of the home. Furthermore, employed women lack the long hours that their mothers devoted to home care. An executive in her early 30s said:

> It finally dawned on me that my mother spent all her time making the house look the way it did. I was wasting a lot of energy and irritation on picking up, trying to be neat, and just decided that it wasn't worth it. [Was that something you consciously decided?] Yes, I consciously decided my home was going to have to be different than the house I grew up in. I had to not only acknowledge that, but also act on it. That meant that if I needed to leave the dirty socks on the floor, so be it. And that I needed to hire someone to come and vacuum once a week.

Another woman, in discussing the same issue, reported a moment of revelation when she allowed herself to believe that "no one ever died of dust balls."

About one third of the women commented on feeling that their mothers had a less stressful life in some respects than their own. The few women in the sample who reported working primarily for financial reasons and felt most ambivalent about having careers were especially likely to express some envy that their mothers had more leisure time. A businesswoman in her upper-30s, who said she would stop working if the family could afford it, remarked: "It seems, at least to me, that my mother had a lot more leisure time than I do. There are times when I would love to just have more time to relax, and do some hobbies, or whatever." For the majority of dual-career wives, however, the costs of being a full-time homemaker outweigh any benefits of a potentially less stressful lifestyle. One woman in her early 40s said:

> My mother's life might have been less stressful, but I'm not so sure. I have a theory about stress that it comes from whatever situation you're in. So for me it's stressful to get out of the house by 8:00 every morning, but maybe for my mother, who was home every morning, it was stressful to get out by noon.

For men, not doing what their fathers did takes multiple forms. Implicit or explicit in the discussions of many men was a view that they no longer occupy the position of *head of household*. A businessman in his early 30s noted:

> My father was clearly the boss of the family. He knew what was coming in and what was going out. He paid all the bills. So there's a big discrepancy there, because I do nothing financially. Joann pays all the bills, makes

almost all the financial decisions. Now that I think about it, that's almost a complete role reversal.

A scientist in his upper-30s remarked:

> My father wanted to dominate the family. I didn't want to do that. I very much wanted to have a dual-career family, very specifically, and have a sense of shared responsibility.

A major change that men discussed was that their fathers had enjoyed the luxury of a full-time wife. Although the majority of the dual-career husbands claimed that they preferred a dual-career marriage over a one-career marriage, there was considerable envy voiced about their fathers' lack of duties around the home. Tom, an academician like his father, discussed this in a partly ironic tone of voice:

> If I had advice for someone in my position, I'd say marry a rich woman who wants to be a housewife, who won't be particularly needy for your time, but likes having you around. I guess that's my mother. She wanted children and to keep the house nice for my father. He had it unbelievably easy, I feel. He just didn't have many of the stresses and time pressures that I have in my life. He worked very hard, and was extremely productive, but contributed much less to the practical aspects of the house. I'm a little jealous. I think that'd be nice. And most mothers I knew were like my mother, and fathers were like my father.

A lawyer in his early 40s stated:

> My dad would come home at 7:30 or 8:00, with the kids in bed or doing homework, and my mother would have dinner prepared. He was a wonderful man, but in a nutshell, he didn't have to do any shitwork, and that makes a big difference to one's feeling of harrassment.

These discontinuities that emerge from *not* doing what parents did revolve around the traditional family roles for men and women. For women, these changes pertain to their not reproducing the full-time devotion of their mothers to home and family. For men, the discontinuities, which arise from their wives' careers, involve the dual-career husbands not replicating their fathers' status as sole breadwinners with full-time housewives at home.

VIEWS HELD BY THE FAMILIES OF ORIGIN

Against this backdrop of major intergenerational change, how do the participants' families of origin view their dual-career marriages? It is important to remember that this study examines only ways in which the dual-career spouses *think* that their marriages are perceived by their parents and families.

Parents

The participants described a wide variety of parental reactions to their dual-career marriages. At one extreme are the parents of a man in his early 30s: "They just see dual-career families as the way the world turns now." At the other end of the continuum are the parents of a woman in her upper-30s: "They feel confused why I would work since my husband has a good job." The parents of an academic in her early 40s also lie at the latter end of this continuum:

> It's hard to know if anyone in my family has taken me seriously. I guess they're proud of me, but neither my mother nor father takes me very seriously. They're happy I'm married, they like Joe, I think they're relieved I'm taken care of. They don't really believe I could take care of myself. They would probably deny that, but I don't think they believe that I, or any woman, could or should take care of herself.

Joe, her husband, corroborates this view of her family:

> Her family has problems with it. They're more traditionally oriented than my family. They get a kick out of her successes—sure they're proud of her—but they have a hard time with her as an independent female. Especially her father gives her shit about it—the shit gets more subtle as time goes on, but still . . . So there's a good deal of ambivalence. When she got married, her father made comments about how now she could be a more traditional woman.

Children constitute a central issue in the relationships between most of the dual-career spouses and their parents. With few exceptions, the dual-career spouses said parents felt it was crucial to have children. It is important to recognize that only dual-career couples with children are included in the study. A physician in his early 30s spoke of his family's view of their dual-career marriage: "If we weren't turning out how they would like, then there might be more tension about our dual careers. In particular, if we hadn't started a family, I think both sets of parents would pressure Mary to stop working." A scientist in her upper-30s, with a young child, talked of her parents' strong message that a career was no substitute for children: "They have always given a complete double message: It's very good to have a PhD from you, but you better give us a grandchild as well."

Beyond having children, the question of who takes care of them occupies a central position in the reactions of parents to the dual-career marriage. Surrogate caretakers and day-care centers are alien in both concept and practice to almost all parents of the dual-career spouses. At a basic level, many parents of the participants question whether it is possible to combine career and motherhood. Mothers in particular were seen as doubting whether it was feasible, let alone desirable, for a woman to have a career and children. Typically, the focus of this debate is the well-being of the child. A businesswoman, now in her early 40s, gave birth to her child while she was in business school:

> My mother took a while to be convinced that you could have a career with children. She used to bombard me with, "What about the baby? What about the baby?" I would say, "She's fine, she's at the day-care center." After a while, she saw she *was* fine.

Many people reported that the tension about day care dissipated only as the evidence accrued: that is, the grandparents could observe that the grandchild was indeed "turning out okay." A psychologist in her mid-30s said that she was grateful to have that evidence: "My mother had no confidence that I could choose a person who was capable of taking care of my infant. But the kid is a terrific kid, so she can't quarrel with what we do."

The clear focus of the parents of the dual-career spouses is on the woman: Should she stay home with the child? Can she handle the combination of career and motherhood? Of the two spouses, the wife with a career represents the more blatant defiance of tradition. In this matrix of parents and offspring, the relationship of mothers to daughters seems the most charged vector. An architect in his early 40s commented:

> There's a much bigger generation gap between mother to daughter than father to son in our age group, because it's been such a radical change for women. Although there is a very perceptible change between me and my father in the balancing of home and work, somehow that's an easier one to comprehend. It's not like a complete reversal, which I think the professional woman, daughter of the housewife, is. It's almost a repudiation of a previous generation.

However, there were also several dual-career spouses who noted that their parents were increasingly aware and appreciative of the dual-career husband's role in child care. An administrator in his upper-30s remarked: "My parents accept the idea of dual careers, although they worry that my child may get less of her mother's attention than in their experience. At the same time, they're impressed that she gets more of my attention."

Aside from issues concerning children, many parents of dual-career spouses have broader questions about the viability of the dual-career lifestyle. They perceive, in the dual-career family, a dramatically different way to allocate time and a quickened pace of life. In particular, mothers of dual-career women seem concerned that the couple, and especially the daughter, does too much. A woman lawyer in her mid-30s described:

> My mother thinks we are certifiable! (laugh) She is so proud of me, and is reliving her life through me. And on the other hand, she vacillates. She comes to visit, and our house is a complete zoo. The time that her ambivalence was most clear was when I was pregnant. She was devastated by what I was doing to my body and this fetus, by being under so much pressure. And it was a real conflict for her. On the one hand, she had encouraged me my whole life to "go for it," and now she was saying, "How can you do all this?"

As women reflected on their mothers' perceptions of their dual-career lifestyle, the issue again emerged of how a working woman's relationship to her home differs from her mother's. A woman academic in her early 30s stated:

> My family doesn't comprehend what I do, and what it means in terms of time and commitment. What they see is that we hire a cleaning lady. My mother feels that *she* never had to hire a cleaning lady. She doesn't understand that I spend my evenings writing papers and grants.

For many parents, the dual-career marriages of their offspring represent their most direct connection to the rapidly changing world in which women pursue careers even if they have young children. Just as the attitudes and behaviors of the dual-career spouses have not remained static over time, so too have their parents undergone shifts in expectations. A man in his early 40s commented:

> My mother has undergone an interesting evolution, from thinking this is a crazy idea, and why didn't we spend more time with the children, and why didn't we come visit her more often. But she comes and visits, and that helps her realize how frantic our lives are and how relatively capable we are of dealing with it. And I think she is now able to understand that this is an alternative to the way of living she's used to.

Despite the mothers' concerns about child care, housekeeping, and the hectic pace of dual-career life, two thirds of the women felt their mothers had generally supported, if not encouraged, them in education and career. Those women in the older generation who had by-passed careers with regret or resentment tended to be proud and supportive of their daughters' work. As a somewhat ironic outgrowth of their own career longings, some mothers seemed, according to their daughters, to underestimate the challenges and complexities inherent to juggling career and motherhood. A physician in her upper-30s felt that her mother did not appreciate the pulls that she felt between work and children:

> My mother really wanted me to have a career. After my daughter was born, I agonized about going back to work. My mother really pushed me to go back. She didn't empathize with how hard it was for me to leave my baby, since she had never left us.

However, many women said their mothers undermined their confidence in themselves and were unsupportive of their professional efforts. An executive in her early 40s said:

> My mother was not a role model. It took me so long to realize I had a vocation, that I was a working mother. And one of the outcomes of this was that I am constantly discussing options with my daughters, giving them confidence that there are so many things they can do. My mother never did that.

Importantly, mothers who worked did not necessarily endorse work for their daughters more than mothers who were not employed: The crucial variable was the reason for their employment. Mothers who worked by choice (and this frequently took the form of volunteer work) tended to support the daughters' work. However, mothers who worked out of economic necessity often had difficulty understanding why women would choose to work. Marla described that her mother, who was widowed and therefore worked to support her family, felt that if work were not financially necessary, it would be better for mothers not to work: "Even though my mother worked, she wishes in some ways that I didn't. I know that's especially true now, since I became a mother."

In general, then, the dual-career spouses perceived the strongest reactions from mothers to daughters. The dual-career wives perceived their mothers as concerned with those dimensions of domestic life on which the daughters were spending less time than their mothers: child care primarily and the home secondarily. The dual-career husband's parents rarely saw *his* lifestyle as an issue but rather focused on his wife's—a dimension to which we now turn.

In-Laws

The daughter's career redefines woman's role not only for her own family but also for her husband's family. Mothers-in-law sometimes responded to the woman's career with support and encouragement, especially if they had experienced but not actualized their own career aspirations. A woman in her upper 30s commented: "His parents, especially his mother, have been real rooters for us. His mother is a bright, independent woman, and had a lot to do with Dave's expectations for a wife." However, support for women having careers is distinguished from behaviors and attitudes fostering men's increased involvement in the household, as a woman in her mid-30s pointed out:

> His mother never went to college, but she really feels it's very important for women to have careers. On the other hand, she provided a very traditional home, not only for Sam's father, who did practically nothing around the house, but also for her sons, who never learned to cook or clean or do things involved in day-to-day living. So Sam didn't know how to do any of that.

Another frequent reaction of mothers-in-law, especially among women who did not have daughters of their own with careers, was apathy or indifference. A musician in her upper-30s commented that her mother-in-law "could give two cents" that she has a career. Several women echoed a businesswoman who stated that her husband's family "never took what I did seriously."

About one third of the women felt that their working status was a source of conflict with their mothers-in-law. A businesswoman in her mid-30s reported: "It's always been a point of contention with his mother that I'm a working mother, and she wasn't. So that makes us very different." The conflict often centered, as with their own mothers, around child care. A scientist in her upper-30s stated: "I think Scott's mother is proud, but she also doesn't think this is the way a child should be raised." A number of women noted that their in-laws objected not to the dual-career wife's pursuit of a work life but to the degree of her involvement in her career. An academic in her early 30s stated: "His parents think it's fine that I have a job, but they don't like it or understand it if I have to go back to work in the evening."

In this relationship between the woman and her in-laws, the husband's sisters often played a mediating role. If the husband has sisters with careers, then the dual-career wife does not represent his family's first or primary exposure to the possibility of dual-career families. Interestingly, however, a number of women perceived that their mothers-in-law supported their career pursuit in a way that they seemed not to endorse it for their own daughters. Perhaps these older women have become open to the idea of women having careers in the abstract and can be relatively supportive and unthreatened by it as long as it does not apply to their own daughters. A son's wife having a career signifies change, but it may feel one step removed compared to a daughter's career. A businesswoman in her early 30s noted:

> My mother-in-law doesn't want *her* daughter to work, but she has seemed positive regarding my work. She offered from the outset to provide child care, if we wanted. So I leave my baby with my mother-in-law and sister-in- law, who is over there with her own baby. And then I go off to work.

Siblings

In order to understand the place of the dual-career couples within their families, it is important to look within as well as across generations. Perhaps equally as impressive as the differences between generations is the broad diversity *within* a generation of a family.[6] The reactions of siblings often echoed those of parents. A scientist in his early 40s stated: "We perplex my sister, who is in a one-career marriage. She doesn't understand our hectic life."

Siblings potentially can render a significant influence on the parents' view of the dual-career marriage. When dual-career marriage is normative or universal among siblings, parents seem to accept it as the current status quo. An executive in his early 30s stated: "All my siblings work and are married to spouses who work, so my parents just assume that everyone works now. In fact, all my cousins are in dual-career marriages too."

Of those spouses who had siblings, half of the women (as contrasted to one quarter of the men) had families in which all siblings were in dual-career marriages. The majority of these women came from families with all daughters. The high incidence of dual-career marriages in families with all daughters may relate to the view of many of these women that they were raised like sons and that their parents,

---

[6] The men and women in the sample fell roughly into the same patterns of birth order. About half were either first-born or only children, one quarter were middle children, and one quarter were youngest children.

and particularly their fathers, were highly invested in their achieve-ments.[7]

About one fifth of the participants came from families in which some but not all of the siblings were now in dual-career marriages. In the families of one half of the men and one quarter of the women, no other sibling was in a dual-career marriage.

Few dual-career spouses had discussed their dual-career status with siblings, and participants typically sounded more unclear and hypo-thetical about their siblings' perceptions of their dual-career family than they did about their parents' views. A lawyer in his mid-30s stated:

> My brother and sister grew up at a time when dual- career families were increasingly common. And yet Jane and I are the only dual-career family. My siblings are tolerant; I don't know if they're supportive. We've never talked about it.

Differences between two-career and one-career families may carry more emotional charge among relatives within rather than across generations, for they represent different choices made by people who allegedly faced comparable options. A wide range of complicated reactions was described among siblings: support, competition, disap-proval, and envy.[8] An academic in his mid-30s said: "I think my siblings feel intimidated by Joann's career. I don't know if they also feel disapproving." The sources of disapproval noted among siblings stemmed primarily from two sources. First, again, was child care: Sisters and sisters-in-law who did not work outside the home were often critical or suspicious of day care or surrogate care for children. Second, brothers in one-career marriages often conveyed the view that, ideally, women need not work outside the home. A museum curator in his mid-30s commented: "I'm the only one of my siblings in a dual-career marriage. My brother likes that he earns enough that his wife doesn't need to work."

Impact of Familial Views

What effect do the current views of parents and in-laws have on the dual-career spouses? To the extent that the parental views have col-

---

[7] Evidence supports this view that daughters in families without sons tend to receive strong encouragement for achievement from their parents and especially from their fathers (Lynn, 1980).

[8] Interestingly, many dual-career spouses described virtually identical emotions in their relationships with siblings in one-career marriages as in their social relationships with nonemployed women and one-career couples. They often viewed these relation-ships as difficult and tense. As is described later, dual-career couples reported that they socialize almost exclusively with other dual-career couples.

ored the views of the dual-career spouses, we can expect that they will carry considerable significance. For example, if parental ambivalence toward women's careers or surrogate child care has been internalized, then clearly an impact is felt within the marriage. As discussed previously, expectations that originated in the childhood family sometimes persist in the current dual-career marriage. We might conjecture that continuing support of the parents for these traditions serves a reinforcing function. In times of transition and change and on issues about which people may feel ambivalent and unsure, parental support for one side or the other may tip the scales.

Both men and women who felt their dual-career lifestyle was unsupported or misunderstood by their parents expressed regret over this difference. In general, however, the dual-career spouses said their parents exerted relatively little influence over how they currently conducted their lives. This may not be surprising in the context of the considerable geographic distance between most of the couples and their parents. Perhaps this degree of change in the space of a single generation would not have been possible if people stayed close to home—literally as well as figuratively.

GENDER-LINKED EXPECTATIONS ABOUT WORK AND FAMILY

We have seen that expectations from the family of origin about work and family are brought to the dual-career marriage. These develop in early childhood, out of experiences and observations of what life is and fantasies of what life could be. However, expectations brought to work and marriage evolve over time in multiple layers and dimensions. We have observed that dual-career couples' lives are not mirror images of early parental examples. Some expectations are born later, from intellectual thought, additional experiences, and continuing fantasies. These later-developing expectations may be layered on rather than replace prior expectations.

For the current discussion on expectations, it is important to place the participants at least roughly along a timeline of sociocultural change. In 1963, Betty Friedan published *The Feminine Mystique*, an event that many date as the birth of the modern women's movement. In 1963, the participants were between 10 and 20 years old. Therefore, the oldest participants generally entered college and (if they married early) marriage with a prefeminist mentality. For these couples, we predict that women's pursuit of high-commitment careers and the concomittant changes in marriage typically occurred after the wedding. Many of the younger participants lived through a prefeminist childhood but encountered the possibility of women's careers while still in adolescence or college. Hence, we expect that many of them entered marriage with an understanding that both spouses would work. However, as noted previously, these later feminist-era expectations probably added to rather than replaced earlier expectations. Furthermore, expectations that emerge from changed values and abstractly derived ideals may differ in immediacy, specificity, and perhaps power from early parental role models.

Each partner brings to a marriage expectations not only about his or her own role but also about his or her spouse's role. Taken together, these images for self and spouse form an internal portrait of how married life should be. Expectations can exert a powerful influence over how one conducts and experiences one's life. When one's life diverges from expectations, the potential exists for intrapersonal dissonance or perhaps for unexpected pleasure. The degree to which spouses' expectations converge or diverge can be expected to affect the degree of marital conflict and satisfaction.

The expectations brought to a marriage are extremely complex and infinitely varied among individuals. At the risk of oversimplification, let us extract from these subtle, multifaceted expectations a simple, bold pair of gender-linked expectations about work and family in our society. These expectations form a powerful legacy that dual-career spouses inherit, whether they later embrace or transform them. This pair of expectations can be summarized as:

Work is more important to men than women.
Family is more important to women than men.

This gender-linked dichotomy of work and family provides a complement of deeply ingrained beliefs and traditions about how the work and family spheres should combine. To the extent that the dual-career marriage represents an attempt to rewrite the script of traditional marriage, this pair of expectations encompasses much that requires revision. To the extent that the dual-career marriage resembles the traditional marriage, this pair of expectations encapsulates much of the intergenerational continuities.

Men and Work

Husband as Sole Breadwinner. The most orthodox subscription to the belief that men belong in the world of work in a way that women do not is embodied in the classic role division of male breadwinner and female homemaker. As discussed, the majority of both the men and women in the sample grew up in families in which only the father worked outside the home. However, by the time they married, only one quarter of the couples in the sample expected that the wife stay at home with the children while the husband went to work. Let us begin by considering factors that are associated with the endurance of this expectation at the time of marriage.

As predicted, the age of the dual-career spouses is negatively related to their expectations that women work continuously outside of the home. The older couples in the sample were more likely than their younger counterparts to have grappled *within* the context of their marriage with the most basic issue of the wife's involvement in the world of work. These older couples illustrate the adjustment required of both men and women in the wake of changing gender roles. Jane, a woman in her early 40s, stated:

> Rob and I shared expectations of what a woman and a man should do. My decision to work—and to demand that he help out in the household—threw a monkey wrench in for *both* of us. I did not want my work to be a hobby, which is hard for him, still. It's not what he bargained for, or what he had envisioned his life to be.

Several men in the upper end of the age spectrum reported feeling like "the game rules changed halfway through." Rob, Jane's husband, articulated this feeling that the terms of the "bargain" had been altered:

> I remember saying to Jane about 10 years into the marriage that I felt like the game rules had been changed on me. I hadn't changed, but society had. And now I was being asked, or rather told, that I needed to be different. I married with an expectation that I would come home and find dinner on the table and that I would provide the money. My wife's end of the bargain was to take care of the house and kids. So it's been hard. I felt like the rug was pulled out from under me.

These older couples experience themselves as a transitional cohort on the cusp of a new era. They look ahead at older couples and see one-career marriages or women who returned to work after raising children; they see younger couples behind them entering marriage expecting a dual-career lifestyle. A man in his upper-30s noted:

> I think this is a generational issue. People who are 10 years younger than us don't make the same kinds of choices as we do, or it's more natural. The men assume the women will be in career roles, and the women

assume they'll be in career roles. And therefore they don't have the built-in conflicts that we had. For us, those things are a matter of choice and not natural. And I think that things that are a matter of choice are more harsh and more tense. There's a lot of wondering if it's a good choice, the right choice. It's more of a fight to determine if what seems the right thing *is* the right thing.

In addition to age, social class of one's family of origin bears some association to expectations of a one- rather than two-career marriage. Sons and daughters of middle- to upper middle-class families tended to have mothers who were well-educated and to be exposed to, sometimes involved in, the women's movement. In contrast, men and women from working-class backgrounds felt they had little or no exposure to role models for or ideology about women having career ambitions. Several of these dual-career spouses emphasized that the wife worked for financial reasons rather than for self-fulfillment. A man in his early 30s from a working-class background said:

When we started out, both of us thought that I would have the more successful career . . . or should I say the only career. That was the only way we knew things went. I guess I'm surprised how it's turned out. I would have expected her to leave work after the child was born. But when it came time, we still needed her income.

Two issues appear most influential in the shift of expectations from a one-career to a two-career marriage. First, women experienced a continuing desire to work after the birth of children or a renewed desire to work after a period away from the workforce. As is seen in the following chapter, women often increased their commitment to work over time, as it changed from a job into a career in external form and internal meaning. Women also described the influence of the women's movement on their decision to pursue a career. Second, for a few couples, the perceived need for the wife's financial contribution to the family superseded her continuing desire to be a full-time mother and housewife.

This subgroup of couples who expected one-career marriages provides an opportunity to examine how people experience a discrepancy between expectations and reality. Responses to the gap between expectations and reality often depend on who initiated the change and why. Men who did not expect a dual-career marriage typically experienced themselves, at least initially, as passive, unwelcoming recipients of the dual-career status. Whether the wife's work was prompted by her desire to continue her employment or by financial reasons, the man did not actively initiate the dual-career status. For these men, whose expectations to be the sole breadwinner were intact at the time of the marriage, wife employment presented a challenge to their sense of masculinity. Jack, a man in his upper-30s who grew up in a working-class family, perceived the provider role as integrally linked to his pride and sense of manhood:

> I did not want my wife to work after our child was born—because the macho men in my family would never permit it. They'd say, what's the matter, don't you make enough money to let your wife stay home and take care of the kid? And no, I didn't make enough money to let my wife stay home and take care of the kid. I agonized over it. But it was a fact of life. I'm not in the minority anymore—but back then, not a lot of wives worked, and it bothered me a lot.

A wife's decision to pursue a career therefore affects her husband's experience of his work role in a potentially profound way: He is no longer sole breadwinner. What happens to this conflict between internal expectations and external reality? For some men, a shift in expectations followed the external changes, with the result that the wife's work became more acceptable. Jack, for example, spoke of his increased ability to take vicarious pleasure in his wife's accomplishments and to take pride in being married to a successful woman. These shifts in attitude may result from efforts to reduce cognitive dissonance and to increase consistency between expectations and reality. However, some men said the dissonance created by the gap between expectations and reality has not yielded fully to *reframing* and *reattribution*. The wish for a change in reality persists among these spouses. For example, soon after Jack described his increased appreciation of his wife's career, he responded without pause to a question about what aspects of his dual-career marriage he would most like to change: "I'd love to make it a single-career family: to earn enough money so that she could stay home, be a mom, go to the country club, like the Donna Reed show. That would make me feel great."

Those women who choose to work describe a shift in expectations. In contrast to their expectations at the outset of their marriages, they now expect that work is a part of their life. A female executive in her early 40s commented with pleasure: "I expected that I would have children and play bridge for the rest of my life. And now look at me!" However, the few women who described financial reasons as the sole motivation for their employment continued to experience personal dissonance between expectations and reality. Similar to the men discussed previously, they felt themselves passive rather than active players in their employment.

People may not realize the extent of dissonance created for their spouses by the gap between expectations and reality. Julia, a woman in her upper-30s who supported the family while her husband was a student, spoke of this:

> When I was working and he was going to school, he had a lot of trouble. I didn't know that. He wanted to go to school, but somehow it wasn't right for a woman to be supporting a man who should be supporting his family. We finally got to a point where we could talk about that. He's a really open, liberal kind of person, and it was kind of shocking to me to find out that it was as much of a problem for him as it was. I would never have expected that. So I realized that he still has some firm, traditional ideas about roles.

Let us look now at the counterexpectation: that is, that the man would *not* be the sole breadwinner. The majority of women and men in the sample expected at the time of marriage that both spouses would be employed. Approximately half of the men reported that they had a clear desire to marry a woman with work interests. A man in his early 30s described why he sought a dual-career marriage:

> In school, I remember thinking very consciously that I wanted to marry a woman with career aspirations, because of the monetary advantages and the type of woman who had ambitions. And I don't mind the strains that are introduced because she has a successful career. In some ways, I think the strains would be greater if she were—I don't want to say *simply* a housewife—but if her energies were more directed towards the home. I don't have a good idea of why. It has to do with her getting a lot of approval and recognition and appreciation outside the house, so she needs less of it from me. I have the feeling otherwise she would be drawing on me more than she does for those things.

Many men—mostly younger—spoke of making a conscious choice between women who had or intended to have a career and those who were focused primarily on home and family. In addition, several older men noted a desire from the outset to be with a woman who would be active in the world outside the home, either at a job or volunteer work, although they tended not to have expected that she would pursue a continuous career. A man in his early 40s described an early sense of wanting a "stimulating, active wife":

> When I first started seeing Meg, I was dating another woman. I remember very clearly having a conversation with this other person where she said that all she really wanted to do with herself was get married and raise a

family. And I remember that conversation as the beginning of the end of that relationship. I never had to have that kind of conversation with Meg, because it was clear that she had a lot of energy and wanted to do all kinds of things, even if it wasn't clear what form that would take.

In summary, then, for only a minority of the couples does the *fact* of wife employment run counter to the expectations that they held at the time of their marriage. We now turn to a question of degree rather than kind with respect to the traditional association of work with men and here find a far more pervasive expectation of the dual-career couples in the study.

Husband's Career as Primary. An expectation of two careers is not synonomous with an expectation of two equal careers. Among the couples who entered marriage expecting that the wife as well as the husband would engage in some form of paid work, a common under-lying assumption was that his career would be more important than hers. The ways in which his career might retain salience took many forms: time, success, money, and prestige.

Older couples were more likely than younger ones to have entered the marriage with this assumption. Laura and John, a businesswoman and an architect in their early 40s, subscribed explicitly to the expec-tation that his career would matter more, would utilize more time, and would earn more money. Laura described:

> I was going to say that my career is subservient to his, although those aren't the exact words that I want to use. But what I mean is mine is somewhat secondary to his. In terms of income, he makes a lot more. I don't know if maybe it's because I graduated from college just a little too soon to take advantage of the women's movement. I see myself as both a homemaker and a career person. I don't see myself trying to make Senior V.P. in 10 years, and I do see John in that position.

John depicted similar expectations:

> I automatically assumed when we started out that I would be more successful than her. And that's how it's been. If she were as totally committed to her career as I am to mine, we'd have to work some things out. I'm given a lot more leeway by her than I would give to her, like coming home late and grumpy. If she had to do the same things, I'm not so sure that I'd be happy with it. If she called me up, as I do her, and said she couldn't get home till 1:00 a.m., I would question the value of that, because her career is not as significant. We've accepted the fact that my job, at least functionally, is different than hers.

The match between long-standing expectations and reality can help minimize intrapersonal and interpersonal conflict. In addition, this convergence of expectations and reality can be a source of satisfaction. Laura continued:

> I grew up in a family where the expectation was that a husband would have a successful, accomplished career. I don't know what it would be like to be married to someone whose career was less successful than mine. It fulfills a lot of my expectations. I expected to grow up and marry a man who was as successful as my father. So the fact that John is as successful as my father is a strength in our marriage, because it fulfills an expectation. It's a reinforcing kind of thing.

The allocation of time (a pivotal issue in the dual-career marriage to which we return later) comprises a key way in which differential importance of the two careers is established and maintained. For many, as for Laura and John, relative salience of careers was reflected in terms of daily and weekly allocation of time: who worked more hours, who returned to the office in the evening or on weekends, and who accommodated their schedules to child-care demands. In four couples, the differential allocation of time to work was formalized: One spouse worked part time (two thirds time or more). In three of these couples, the woman worked part time, and in one couple, the man worked part time.[9] Although no firm conclusions can be drawn from this small subsample, some speculations can be made. In general, the reduction in work hours was at least partly designed to reduce role strain and manage more effectively the multiple tasks of childrearing, home management, and career. To some extent, working less than full time in our society carries a message about the salience of work in an individual's—and a couple's—life. However, as we see later, the majority of dual-career wives reduced their work hours to some extent in order to accommodate children. Hence, part-time employment represented a more explicit expression of a pattern that was common among the sample as a whole.

Another expression of the differential salience of spouses' careers is a view of men's careers as essential and women's careers as optional. Both the men and the women had devoted much time and effort to establishing themselves in their careers. However, a common percep-

---

[9] It needs to be recognized that part time means very different things in different fields. Hence, a physician working 80% time still worked considerably more than 40 hours per week. Some law firms that have now implemented part-time options for new mothers highlight the multiple meanings of part time in the modern work world: part time means 9:00 to 5:00.

tion was that the woman's career was not a necessity in the way the man's was and that women could afford psychologically and financially not to be employed. Half of the women said it would be conceivable (although not desirable) for them to assume the full-time role of motherhood. Even among those women who always assumed they would have a career, there was frequent acknowledgement that a career for women in general, and for them in particular, still felt more discretionary than it did for men. For many women, the traditional female role of full-time homemaker represented a safety net should their careers founder. A female lawyer in her mid-30s who felt that she had been career-oriented "forever" stated:

> I feel sorry for men, because a woman can always be a mother, and can really enjoy motherhood. If tomorrow something happened to my career, I can always say, well, I have motherhood, I still have a role. Whereas with men, work is totally important to them.

Sarah, a highly successful businesswoman in her upper-30s, has risen steadily and rapidly through the ranks. Her husband, Jeff, felt frustrated with his career having reached a ceiling in terms of promotion and salary. She commented:

> There's a lot more tolerance in society for women to become professional people or not; the whole range of options is there. There's not the same range for men. The same old rigid stereotypes exist that were there when men like Jeff were growing up. The expectation is that he will be the breadwinner, have a profession, have a new car, take care of his wife, whether she works or not. All those expectations still hold for men in a very real sense. I understand that more men do dishes now and that kind of stuff, but professional expectations are as strong as ever for men. They're a lot looser and more generous for women.
>   So Jeff grew up in that. And he's unable to get out of those stereotypes, those hard-driving male stereotypes. I don't think it's the same thing as not being able to allow women to be successful. He feels no choice: He *needs* to be successful. And he's never going to change that. You read about women breaking stereotypes, and men doing more fathering. But I don't think this is getting written about.

What happens when expectations about career salience do not materialize? It was difficult for people to articulate what the gap between expectations and reality felt like. Often, it was described as vaguely but profoundly unsettling. Marlene, a woman in her upper-30s, spoke of "waking up" early in her marriage to a reality that differed significantly from her expectations, and feeling unhappy with it:

I grew up in a family where you were supposed to grow up, get married and have children. You went to college because it was socially the thing to do—it was interesting, you met nice friends there, and that was that. So here I was with a Ph.D., working while my husband stayed home to work on his thesis and take care of our new baby—and I didn't like it. This role reversal, well, it didn't fit at all with what I knew.

From this point of dissonance, equilibrium is sought in several ways. If spouses agree that his career should be primary, they often can tailor their lives to accomplish this. For example, Marlene and her husband invested their pooled energies into his career progressing and moving onto center stage, and she de-escalated her own career growth.

Alternatively, reality may remain unchanged and expectations may be altered, leading to a reduction in dissonance. Although both husbands and wives faced considerable challenge in accepting her career as more salient or successful than his, ideological commitments to gender equality helped provide a positive attribution for the situation.

A third outcome is that people live with dissonance, with the tensions inherent to life not going as planned. The dissonance may be shared. When both spouses had expected the husband's career to be preeminent, the effects of a more successful wife can prove difficult for both spouses and for the marriage. Alternatively, expectations of the spouses regarding career salience may differ from the outset or may diverge over time. Often, the wife's expectations regarding career salience shifted as she became increasingly committed to and successful in her career. Despite the husband's acceptance of her career in general, it was often difficult for him to perceive her career on par with or more advanced than his. As we see in chapter 3, often the dual-career wife also felt ambivalent about her success outpacing his. If her career equaled or surpassed her husband's in success or prestige, she too experienced intrapersonal dissonance between expectations and reality, as well as often fearing for the effects on her husband and on her marriage.

One quarter of the couples entered marriage with the counterexpectation that the man's career would be no more salient or important than the woman's. Younger couples were more likely than older ones to bring this expectation into their marriages. They were more likely to accept women having high-commitment, high-success work lives comparable to their husbands. Similarly, older couples who married later (in their 30s) were more likely to expect equal career status. These individuals appeared to have undergone considerable evolution of expectations prior to marriage. In addition, women who married later tended to be firmly established and invested in their careers rather than being in the formative stages where ultimate salience of the career may be uncertain.

Women and Family

Regardless of whether spouses expected the wife to be a primary worker *outside* of the home, they almost invariably anticipated that she would be the primary worker *inside* of it. The expectation that work is more important for men than women is not totally independent from the expectation that home is more important for women than men. However, these two basic expectations prove not to be mirror images. In particular, some spouses expected that they would have comparable investments in their careers but still expected that they would have differential investments in the home. One husband and wife in their early 30s worked comparable jobs at high-powered New York firms and hence appeared symmetrical along the dimension of work. However, their attainment of identical MBA degrees did not challenge their assumption that she was in charge of the home. Marcy described their early years following business school:

> For the first six years of our marriage, there were probably only 5 or 6 times when he got home before me. Now that meant I got home at 8 p.m. and he got home at 8:30, but still the lights were on, the table was set, and dinner was cooking on the stove when he came in. It must have come from how my mother ran a household, when she spent full time on that. I thought I had to do it all.

Why do women believe they will perform the majority of the domestic work in addition to their careers outside of the home? Many women expressed a need or desire to maintain some primacy over childrearing. More explicit than many was Cindy, a physician in her mid-30s, who had decided to scale back her work hours:

> I never really wanted him to be home more. I think it has to do with competitiveness around the children. I want him to work more and carry more of the financial burden, so that I can be with the kids. Ultimately, that's a fairly traditional view I have, isn't it? It's fine with him. If he wanted to be with the kids as much as I did, I would really worry that I would be displaced. As I talk, I'm realizing that it's fine with me that it's been this way—to my sense of being a mother.

Women often described a feeling that, career not withstanding, they needed to continue to perform the traditional roles of wife, mother, and (for many) housekeeper. Typical was a woman in her early 40s who stated:

> I started out with, and probably still have a lot, the feeling that I had to be superwoman: perfect wife, perfect mother, and also work. I wasn't willing to give any of them up. I like things done the way I like them done. I suppose I could have hired someone to come in and do everything, but I also had the fantasy of taking care of my kids and house myself.

Some women were surprised by their attraction to a more traditional pattern than they had expected. A woman in her mid-30s, now working part time, described the unexpected strength of the traditional pulls of motherhood compared to the pulls of her long sought-after career:

> The main change for me has been to realize how much mothering means to me, as compared to career. I always supposed while working towards a career that I would work full time. After my first child was born, I did work full time for a year. I had never thought the pulls of being a mother would be so strong for me. So that's been the main conflict: putting together my expectations or notions of what I was going to do with my career with what I was going to be as a mother.

Much as some men experienced their sense of masculinity as tied to their provider role, some women described a feeling that maintaining primary responsibility for the domestic sphere preserved their sense of femininity. Several women described a way in which their feminine domestic role counterbalanced their masculine work role. Margaret, a mathematician in her mid-30s, spoke of her need to maintain her identity as a woman by retaining primary responsibility for her daughter:

> I know a marriage where the woman is the breadwinner and the man stays home. It would make me uncomfortable. [What about it would make you uncomfortable?] I would fear that I was losing my femininity. I really think I need motherhood, and periods of playing house, to remind myself that I am a woman. Because when you're in a work situation and working with men, well—men are different. They're very competitive; the psychology is totally different. I sometimes feel like I need to become like that to be successful, and that worries me. I need the home and family to keep my identity as a woman, so I don't get sucked into some of the things that these guys do, because success is so important to them. If that was all there were, I would really fear for my femininity.

Spence (1985) suggested that when a person's gender identity is challenged, he or she will engage in gender-role appropriate behavior in order to reaffirm his or her sense of gender to self as well as to others.

The important counterpoint to this reluctance of some women to give up their domestic roles was the resistance of many men to adopt responsibilities in the home. Among the sources of men's resistance to housework and child care is the expectation that domestic tasks are women's work and that men should not have to be concerned with them. Much as giving up the classic male provider role challenged some men's sense of identity, adopting traditionally female roles in the home grated against men's sense of masculinity. As we see in chapter 4, even those couples who now share a large portion of housework and child care tasks tend to preserve the female role of chief executive of the home.

Is age associated with the expectation of home as more important to women, as it was with the expectation of work as more important to men? Interestingly, the expectation of younger spouses for symmetrical work lives was not necessarily mirrored by an expectation for symmetry within the home. Most couples who sought a more egalitarian division of domestic work did so *after* the wedding. Younger spouses seemed only slightly more prone than their older counterparts to expect or enact domestic role sharing at the outset of their marriages. However, younger couples seemed more amenable to ideological and behavioral shifts. Compared to older spouses, younger men seemed less angered by and resistant to their wives' pleas for their increased involvement, and younger women seemed more able to insist on husband involvement and to feel less conflict about not performing the domestic tasks themselves. A man in his early 40s spoke of the difference between the expectations-reality gap for his peers as compared to younger men:

> Our younger friends in their 30s—it's not as much an issue with them regarding sharing housework as it is with us. So most of the men my age complain that the house is not as clean as it should be or the meals aren't cooked. And we're all doing more than we expected to do! We joke about it. Younger men don't complain. They go along with it.

How has the expectation that the home was woman's domain been actualized in the couples' lives? First, many couples allowed reality to match their expectations. Especially if the wife felt invested in performing the domestic tasks, the spouses' expectations that she maintain primary responsibility for the home tended to converge with each other and with reality. Second, if the wife's expectations about domestic work changed, she faced the option of living with the dissonance between her expectations and reality or of striving to change her husband's expectations and their joint reality. Changing deeply ingrained patterns involved a long, iterative process of negotiation and renegotiation that we examine further later. For some men as well as women, expectations shifted over time. Being able to take credit for and pride in the role changes served to reduce distress that might have been caused by the gap. One man, for example, said his own "personal growth" was precipitated by his wife's insistence that he participate more in domestic tasks. Said a lawyer in his early 40s: "I pride myself in being a man who has moved beyond the traditional role—in terms of taking part in the home, cooking, child care. I pride myself in having made choices about trying to have a more equal relationship in the home."

Some spouses did endorse the counterexpectation—that responsibility for the domestic sphere would be shared—from the outset of their marriage. A fantasy expressed by many couples was that if they had "only known beforehand," they could have negotiated things more effectively. Among the most specific routes to knowing beforehand are previous marriages. The spouses who had been married before said their prior experiences had shaped their expectations about sharing responsibility in the domestic sphere. The few previously married men, in particular, reported that they emerged from a phase of single parenting or joint custody with habits in and commitments to active participation in household and child care tasks. A man in his early 40s described:

> With my first wife, I had more expectations that she would provide what my mother provided. Even though she worked, I think I still expected her to carry the bulk of the work in the home. For myself now, that's an inconceivable model. Maybe that comes from being a single parent for all those years. I can't imagine now being married to someone with a career and expecting her to take on all the household work, because I know now what it entails.

However, regardless of expectations, relative parity in the home was rarely achieved without effort and considerable conflict. People used their beliefs and expectations to buttress themselves in their pursuit of parity. A woman in her mid-30s stated: "The squabbles can feel so repetitive. I need to remind myself that I'm fighting for what I think is right." Notably, even when explicit discussion of the expectations had occurred, the traditional patterns proved hard to break. Here are the separate references of a husband and wife to their explicit negotiations:

> She: I felt like I worked really hard before we had kids to get him to realize what would be involved and to make the time that would be required. On

one hand, he didn't want to be an absent father—reacting against his own family background. At the same time, he had a hard time cutting back. He would come home excited about some new opportunity, which meant more work. And my reaction would be, you've got to be kidding, you don't have the time. So it's a constant struggle.

He: Even before we got married, she told me that she was going to make demands on my time—for helping with household, child care. So I've always felt that the feminist liberation or equal time issue was out on the table; the principle of parity has always been there. So in a sense, I'm balanced between a principle that I essentially agreed to when we got married and an ideal amount of time that I would consider appropriate to devote to my work. Every once in a while I find myself thinking, gee, if only I'd had more time at work, I could have . . .

SUMMARY: GENDER, WORK, AND FAMILY: CONTINUITY AND CHANGE

The roles of both dual-career spouses differ from their parents' roles in key ways: The woman has a career and is not a full-time mother, and the man has more involvement in the home and is not a sole breadwinner. These changes in the divisions of work and family, however, do not necessarily mean absolute departures from the basic expectations that work is more primary for men than women and that family is more primary for women than men. These expectations prove resilient, even with the advent of women's careers.

We have observed that the continuities between the generations reflect these traditional associations of work as a more primary domain for men than women and home as a more primary domain for women than men. Women perceive ways in which, careers aside, they are reproducing their mothers' commitment to mothering and, secondarily, to home and family. Men recognize the extent to which they replicate their fathers' commitment to work life and to occupational success.

The gender-linked pair of expectations represents an important core of the dual-career marriage. For some couples and in some aspects of dual-career family life, this gender-linked dichotomy continues to characterize the work-family system. For other couples and in other domains of the dual-career family, the dichotomy is being challenged, and traditional gender scripts are being revised and rewritten.

Chapter 3

Two Careers in Development

How do I think Sally has viewed and influenced my career? I think encouraging is one word to describe it, accepting is another possibility. I think there may also be a little bit of competition between us. We spend a lot of time trying to keep up with each other's progress. I think there have also been times when she, or her career, has been an impediment, and that also works in reverse. When there are two people with careers, mobility is extremely difficult.

—A business executive in his upper-30s

If one career were more successful than the other, and the less successful person felt less important, that would raise conflict in the marriage. If his career were more successful than mine, that would be more acceptable than the other way around. I guess it's a male-female thing. It feels like the disruption of the family would be less than the other way. It just wouldn't bother me—and he'd probably like it!

—A lawyer in her mid-30s

I think Sara and I see eye-to-eye on what will be best for my career, and it's not here in this city. What's unfortunate is that the career dimensions don't match up with the personal dimensions. If I take the best job for me, I could commute back here on weekends. But that has implications for our relationship, and my relationship with the kids, and our having a daily family life. Where Sara and I differ is the weight we give to those dimensions. I give more weight to career factors, and she gives more weight to personal factors, which for her will affect her work as well. It's very tough.

—A scientist in his early 40s

49

Under the roof of the dual-career marriage are housed two careers that evolve, stumble, change, detour, and triumph. These dual developmental trajectories interact in a multitude of ways. They may progress in tandem or in staggered sequence. The spouses may hurt or help each other's careers. The presence of a career-oriented spouse can provide an understanding and helpful colleague; it also can provide a competitor against whom to mark one's progress.

A substantial literature has accumulated on career development. However, strikingly little attention has focused on how spouses' careers influence and interact with each other. This chapter focuses on the complex interaction of two developing careers in one marriage. First, we examine the developmental courses of spouses' careers along several dimensions, including decisions about careers, role models, and perceptions of career progress. Next, we consider the ways spouses foster and hinder each other's careers, encompassing such dimensions as emotional support, domestic assistance, and geographic moves. We explore how and how much husbands and wives talk with each other about their work. Finally, we examine issues of comparison and competition between spouses and the dynamics of a dual-income marriage.

CAREER PATHS

Career Decisions

The opening chapters of the careers of the men and women in the sample read differently. Almost all of the husbands reported that they always knew they would have a career. They described that they and their families assumed that they would select a career and pursue it successfully. Approximately half the men knew their specific career direction before starting college. Of these, approximately half described dreams dating from boyhood of becoming a lawyer, an architect, and so on. A male physician stated: "I certainly knew by the time I was in high school that I would become a doctor. My mother claims it was much earlier: She has a paper I wrote in first grade saying that I was going to be a doctor." About one quarter of the men decided on their career in college and then pursued a relatively linear path. A small minority of the men underwent a series of career changes after college before settling on their current profession. In short, the husbands' career paths emerged early and then followed a linear developmental pattern.

The women presented a more varied picture than their husbands in terms of timing of career selection and developmental course. One quarter of the women, like the majority of men, reported a precollege interest in the field that they ultimately pursued. Even for this subgroup, however, the specific career was often reshaped in a way different than the men, involving not only a honing of the career goal but an upgrading of the ambition. For example, a woman who knew from an early age that she was interested in science changed her aspirations during college from becoming a high school science teacher to acquiring a doctorate in order to work at a university. Another one quarter of the women chose a career direction in college and then pursued it in a relatively linear manner.

In contrast, half the women described a relatively late-developing sense of career. These women reported that they lacked a sense that they had a career even when advancing up the corporate ladder or pursuing a graduate education. Said a woman in sociology:

> I had gone to graduate school and gotten my PhD because I enjoyed sociology in college and it seemed like the next thing to do. Then my advisor in graduate school was working on this government project, and I started working on it as a research assistant. I moved into a more senior position after I got my degree—but still I didn't really think of it as a career! It took another promotion and a few years before I realized, hey, this is serious, this isn't just a job.

A few women expected to take time off from work after they had children and therefore recognized themselves as career women only when they kept working after the birth of their first child. Several women depicted a meandering early career path with a series of jobs that were only sometimes related to each other and that eventually culminated in a recognition of personal ambitions and a career direction. Frequently, this recognition spurred the women to seek a professional or graduate degree that subsequently launched "the real career," as one woman described it. A few women, especially those in business, benefited from expanding career opportunities for women. One woman, for example, planned to take an extended leave from the workforce after her child was born. Shortly after the birth, she was invited to enter a special management training program for women that she felt was "too good to pass up."[10]

---

[10]Hertz (1986) found, in a sample of dual-career business couples, that it was common for women to have moved from low career ambition to greater career aspirations and

In one third of the couples, the wife worked to support the couple while the husband went to graduate school. The wife's own graduate education typically followed his. This pattern is interwoven with the husband determining his chosen career path earlier than his wife. One effect of this pattern was that, for this third of the couples, the husband was more senior in his field than the wife was in hers.

Importance of Careers

With few exceptions, the husbands considered having a career highly important; repeatedly and with little variation, they stated that their careers were extremely important. One man declared: "My career is probably more important than most other things in my life. Well, yes, it *is* more important. It's what I love." In discussing the importance of their careers to themselves, men were likely to associate career, and especially career achievement, with a sense of core identity. One man commented: "My career is extremely important. It's a central feature of my character. [How so?] Basically, I am ambitious in wanting to achieve something, to make an impression." More men than women spoke of wanting to make an impression through their work. Some men spoke of a mission, a responsibility to use their talents productively:

> I guess I'm an achiever, and that's why I couldn't imagine myself without a career. I wanted to do something, and I wanted it to mean something. I felt I'd been given tools: a good education, certain talents and strengths. I felt I needed to find a career that would allow me to use this education and the gifts I had as a person.

The majority of women also felt their careers were extremely important. However, unlike the men, most of the women spontaneously qualified their responses. The women tended to argue that although career mattered, they would adapt if they did not have one or were not successful at it. A female physician in her upper-30s stated:

> Having a career has been absolutely critical. A lot of my ego and satisfaction in life has been wrapped up in having a career. It would

---

commitment because of expanding career programs for women. It appears that this may have been a factor in the career development of women in business but does not seem as salient in other fields.

certainly be hard if I didn't have it. But I'm not saying that if I failed at this career I wouldn't adjust, because I would.

Several women reported that although they now feel their careers are very important, they did not always feel that way. A woman in business stated: "At first, my career wasn't important at all. It was something to do, and something to earn money at. Now, it's extremely important, and it's hard to imagine not having a career." A small minority of the women felt that their careers were *not* important to them. A business-woman in her mid-30s described her career as relatively unimportant to her, other than monetarily:

It was really just chance and fate that things worked out this way, that I've worked all along. It wasn't a strong desire to go out and make a career. The main rewards are financial. I hate to sound like money is everything, but money is the main advantage. I guess maybe working gives me some satisfaction, too.

Role Models

Participants were asked whether their careers had been influenced by role models. In virtually all of the responses, women looked to women and men to men as mentors and models.

For men, the content area of their career was most important in defining the presence or absence of a role model. Three quarters of the men reported having a role model in the content area of their career; for a third of this group their father or another male relative served as the role model. A physician remarked: "I guess I've had two role models. First was my father, who was a doctor. And then I had an influential professor in college, who got me interested in academic medicine." The remaining quarter of the men had not had a role model. They too weighed the question within the content area of their career. Characteristic was a dentist, who commented: "No, I don't think I had a role model. There were no dentists in my family, and I didn't even like my family dentist. I just thought that dentistry was a good field to go into."

In contrast, only one third of the women had a role model. Like the men, women tended to look for role models within the content area of their career. However, women focused on a different dimension: com-bining career and family. A woman in her early 40s stated:

> In grad school, one professor had three children. I was pregnant at the time, so she was a role model. I remember asking her: Is this possible? How do you do it? And she told me to remember it's not the quantity of time you spend with them, it's the quality.

Interestingly, many women did not have extensive relationships with their role models; rather, these women proved important by their very existence. A female physician in her mid-30s reported:

> One summer in college, I worked in a hospital. I met a woman physician, and spoke with her briefly. She was married, had children, and she wasn't weird. That was extremely important to me. I didn't get to know her—but just meeting a normal person who was a woman physician had a big impact. It made me think it was possible to do this.

Two thirds of the women lacked a role model, and they too used the criteria of women who had combined career, marriage, and children. A woman in her early 40s noted:

> I never had a mentor, a role model. The women I met as a graduate student were not married for the most part; they were older, came from a generation where women chose career or family, a different breed of women. And some women seemed just to be waiting till they had children, when they would stop working.

Many dual-career wives described a conscious search for role models. As a result, women who were encountered in school or at work were approached as potential role models in the sea of men. A woman in business stated: "At my first job I worked for a woman. I hoped she could be a mentor. But she was a very difficult woman. I learned a valuable lesson how *not* to be." Unlike the men who, when they had no role model, did not describe the lack as particularly problematic, women often commented on the difficulty inherent in their perceived lack of role models. A woman academic in her upper-30s stated:

> I think that it [not having a role model] is a prime deficiency for women professionals. Very few women my age have really combined children and careers—and women 10 to 15 years older are into covering their asses more than sharing. They've had to fight so hard, and there are so few of them.

Many women described that the lack of female role models made it difficult to resist masculinization within their fields. A physician, for example, spoke of the resistance of medicine to incorporating "female values," and attributed it in part to a lack of "real women, as opposed to masculine women" in positions of power. A businesswoman in her mid-30s commented:

> I don't have a mentor, a female role model. A worry is that I'm becoming more like the men I work with, and losing aspects of myself as a woman that I value most. I know demographically that more and more women are in the work force and in dual-career marriages, but you still feel like a pioneer. There are no women in power out there.

Two other themes that emerged from the women, again in distinction to the men, were the views that women who might be seen as role models have made tremendous sacrifices and have been superstars. A female academic in her upper-30s summarized:

> Who are my possible role models at the university? Women who have made tenure? There aren't too many of them, and none of them are your average everyday woman who has done good. They're all superwomen, and they'll tell you they've really compromised themselves to make it. The men who make it aren't supermen. They're run-of-the-mill guys who have talent and done well without compromising anything in their lives, for the most part. So I see a real problem here for women in this field. One, I can't look to role models that I think are reasonable, and two, all these things I have to do better than the average guy.

Career Progress and Ambitions

When asked about their career ambitions, the majority of men and women described general goals such as continuing to produce quality research or gaining increased recognition in the field. Nearly half of the men, but almost no women, also articulated highly specific goals, such as particular positions they would like to achieve or awards that they would like to win. A substantial number of women struggled to answer the question, as one businesswoman in her mid-30s stated:

> My career goals? That's tough to say. I've had such an eclectic career. I never really figured out, until recently, what career I was pursuing. It seems like this has something to do with my being a woman.

Participants were asked to consider how well their career progress fit their expectations: Was their career where they thought it might be by this point, further along, or not as far along? Women were evenly divided among the three ratings. Men were somewhat less evenly distributed: Over half of the men felt not as far along as they had expected, and the others were divided between feeling as far and farther along. Perhaps men set higher expectations for themselves in their career progress and therefore are more likely to feel that they have fallen short. An additional explanation may be that dual-career husbands are more likely than their wives to have specific, highly articulated ambitions. The men, therefore, may have more precise standards against which to measure their progress and thus a greater likelihood to experience a discrepancy between expectations and actual accomplishments. Men may thus benefit from specific ambitions and goals, but they also risk feeling disappointed when they do not attain these goals. Women may be more flexible in defining and evaluating their career progress, or perhaps they are defending against disappointing themselves. One woman felt that this difference between herself and her husband explained his feeling less far along in his career:

> I don't have a preconceived notion of where I'm going, whereas George does have a long-term plan. One of the effects of that is that he has more of a sense where he'd like to be when, which can increase frustration if that doesn't happen. For me, things just happen when they happen, and so far it's been mostly good things.

Participants also were asked how they thought their spouses would rate their progress. Half of the women and men accurately predicted how far along their spouses viewed their own career progress. Interestingly, however, more than one third of both men and women viewed their spouse as feeling less far along than the spouse had rated him or herself. The reasons are unclear for this tendency, but perhaps it is a subtle manifestation of competition between spouses. Few women and men rated their spouses as feeling further along than the spouses rated themselves.

In contrast to the disparity between current career status and hoped-for progress, a straightforward inquiry about whether the participants think they are successful yielded a nearly universal answer: yes. Responses varied little between men and women, younger and older participants. Definitions of success emphasized peer recognition and respect, professional power, and money. When asked whether they thought their spouses were successful, participants were again nearly unanimous, and they offered comparable definitions of success in the spouses' fields.

SPOUSES AND CAREERS:
FACILITATION AND HINDRANCE

At the heart of a dual-career marriage is the relationship of each spouse not only to his or her own career but also to his or her spouse's career. The interrelationships of women to their husbands' careers and men to their wives' careers are complex, multiple, and dynamic.

Facilitating the Spouse's Career

Participants said their spouses helped their careers on several levels.

Emotional Support. The most commonly cited way in which the spouses helped was by providing emotional support: A majority of men and women said this was a primary way in which the spouses facilitated their career, and most other participants implied that they benefited from spousal support.

Emotional support for one's career took many forms. It involved an underlying support for one's line of work, for one's commitment to succeed, and for the venture of one's career, broadly defined. Job changes often heightened the importance of the spouse's support for the individual's career. A woman in government in her early 30s stated:

> I wouldn't be doing what I'm doing were it not for his support. This job change was a big risk. It would have been a major source of strain if he wasn't for it. I'm sure I wouldn't have had the courage to take the risk if he hadn't said to do it.

Spouses often functioned as emotional sounding boards. The spouses served as willing and interested listeners to trials and tribulations of the job and sometimes offered feedback and advice as consultants. A woman in her mid-30s described:

> Jay has always been there as a support, always sympathetic. When I was at a job where my relationship with my boss was so awful, things got very tense. Jay had to put up with a really depressed person. That was a time he really helped me through. I guess that's when he's been most supportive—at times of crisis, or when I get really depressed.

Domestic Help. Other ways in which spouses helped with careers were different for men and women. One third of the women cited their husbands' help with household work and child care as helpful to their careers, whereas no men pointed to their wives' household and child care work as facilitating their careers. (Perhaps two men were referring indirectly and broadly to this dimension in delineating the wives' provision of "a happy home" and "a solid home base" as aiding their own career development.) In most instances, the husbands' help at home was described as highly appreciated but delimited and exceptional rather than routine. It was during the period when she was writing her thesis, or doing her medical residency, or under deadline pressure on the job, that his contribution to running the household, "above and beyond the call of duty" in one woman's words, facilitated her career. A female lawyer described:

> When I'm on trial, he is the ultimate facilitator. I'm pretty much checked out. My mind is totally preoccupied with the events of the trial. He makes it all happen at home—he takes care of everything. All I have to say is, I start trial tomorrow, and nothing is expected of me.

Financial Support. In contrast, one quarter of the men cited their wives' financial support as helping their career, whereas only one woman referred to her husband's financial support as contributing to her career development. It appears that the traditional provision of domestic services by women and of income by men tends to be taken for granted by the spouses. It is more likely that the out-of-role behavior—men helping out at home, women contributing to the family income—is noted and viewed as helpful by the spouse.

Concrete Input. Women were more likely than men to appreciate concrete contributions of their spouses to their career: Over one third of the women, compared to only two men, said that their spouses had helped in a concrete, work-oriented way. This went beyond the emotional sounding board role to such tasks as editing papers and providing hands-on assistance. One woman in her mid-30s stated:

> Ron helps me write and to sort out my ideas, in addition to helping me sort things out in general, like people I work with and frustrations of the job. If anyone has been my mentor, it's been Ron. And he enjoys it.

Both the men and women in these couples reported that husbands provided this help to their wives. One man in his early 40s identified that this asymmetry was particularly true in the early years of their marriage:

> One way I helped her career was that I helped her get jobs that were good for her, that fit her needs. Some of that probably sounds, and probably

was, paternalistic. That's how we dealt with things in our first years of marriage.

Why might this provision of concrete input be asymmetrical? Perhaps men feel more confident than women in their ability to contribute to their spouse's career. Perhaps women feel more receptive than men to input from their spouse. The asymmetry suggests a hierarchical relationship, placing the man in a position of presumed expertise and authority. This may be a subtle way in which traditional reality prevails: The world of work is still seen as a world that men know better than women.

Career Interests. Several participants, both men and women, acknowledged that spouses had influenced their career direction and interests. For example, an art historian focused on a certain era of drawing because her husband was a collector; a man's pursuit of a career in sociology stemmed originally from his wife's interest in the field. Common interests and professional passions provide a bond between spouses and a way to integrate work and family. When psychic investment in a career extends well beyond the boundaries of the work day, sharing some of that interest with a spouse can prove rewarding and also may lessen tensions that arise from high commitment to work. A businesswoman who views her specialization in real estate as an outgrowth of her husband's career as a city planner described his knowledge as an asset to her career. In addition, however, were she not to share at least some of his interest in cities, conflicts might arise:

A lot of the reason why I went into real estate was that my husband is a city planner. We spend a lot of time looking at cities. Our vacations always revolve around cities and buildings. Other people go to the beach for vacation, we go walk the streets.

In addition to one spouse being drawn to the interests of the other, spouses sometimes developed opinions about and exerted influence over the other's career path. A variety of career paths had been steered at least partly by the spouse: an applied rather than academic career because tenure pressure was too great; business rather than politics because the time demands of a political career would be extraordinary for both spouses; clinical medicine rather than research because of the greater financial and job security. Of course, these inputs into a career ultimately may prove positive or negative; the spouses presented them as positive.

Hindering the Spouse's Career

In addition to the multilayered ways spouses helped each other's careers, women and men indicated a range of ways their spouses had impeded or interfered with their careers. At the most basic level, being married and having a family means that one cannot immerse oneself with total abandon into a career. A woman in her upper-30s commented:

> Well, being married has affected my career. It makes you part of a world that you're not part of when single; you can't be as selfish. And it seems like if I were more selfish, I'd get more work done. So it's not that he has impeded my career so much as I, as a wife and mother, have impeded my own career.

Compared to their discussion of ways their spouses had been facilitative, participants tended to approach the issue of hindrance more tentatively and with some protectiveness. The typical respondent, when asked "How do you think your spouse has impeded or interfered with your career?" began by saying, "I don't think she (or he) has," and then proceeded to clarify, "except when . . ." Interestingly, both men and women were more likely to point to ways in which they had impeded their spouse's career than to ways in which their own career had been hindered by the spouse. For example, although no participant felt that their spouse's lack of emotional support had proved a career impediment, approximately one quarter of both the men and women stated that their inconsistent emotional support of the spouse's career had probably hindered it.

Domestic Tasks.   Women and men often focused on the demands of home in thinking about how their spouses had hindered their career, but they came at the issue from opposite angles. Over half of the women perceived their husbands' lack of help or low level of help with household and child care responsibilities to be the major way in which husbands had hurt their careers. A woman in her middle-30s stated:

> I don't think he has impeded my career. The only way would be an indirect thing, in that he chose a very demanding career also, so that even though he's helpful with our daughter, he doesn't spend a tremendous amount of time with her. If he did, and if he helped out more around the house, I might be more willing or more anxious to work harder and continue to develop my career more. This way, I'm letting it stand still for the time being.

A typical, although not universal, response of women to this situation was to accommodate their own schedules, often involving career compromises. A woman in her upper-30s reported:

> When he began working on the far side of the city, he made it very clear that I was now in charge of the household. If I wanted to delegate responsibilities to someone—a housekeeper, child care person—that was up to me. So the total responsibility of children and home fell into my balliwick. I don't think it impeded my career, but it meant I had a lot more to think about and deal with. We discussed it at length: he had a longer commute, I was close to home, so it was logical that I would be in charge of the home. I began to resent delegating everything at home, so I began to let go of work to do more things at home.

Women frequently couched their spouses' hindrance of their careers in terms of the husband's "not being as involved as he might be" in home and childcare. Nearly half the men, on the other hand, considered their careers to have been impeded by their wives' requests for their increased involvement in home and child care. A man in his early 40s stated:

> It seems clear to me that if I weren't called on to be a chauffeur from day care twice a week that I would be staying later in the office. There's no doubt in my mind that it's had an impact on my work productivity. How could it not? But I understand that one of us has to do it.

Although the male and female versions of this issue appear in conflict, some participants were able to see both sides of the coin at once. A man in his upper-30s stated:

> She differs greatly from me in her perception of how much time I need to work. She insists that I be home in time for dinner with the kids, or to help make dinner. And then I bargain with her to "buy time": like if I do something extra with the family during the week, I'll steal time during the weekend to work.

At the same time, he recognized that his determination to work as much as possible has probably impeded his wife's career development: "If I were not as ambitious and driven about my work as I am, then she might be less inclined to be the very enthusiastic and conscientious mother that she is." The different approaches of men and women to this issue of domestic work are revealing. They reflect the power of the expectation that the home is woman's domain, and that therefore the man is "helping out" when he contributes.

The Two-Person Career. Many husbands and wives noted that they had not helped each other's careers in traditional ways, such as hosting dinner parties, accompanying the spouse to work-related events, or social networking. When there are two careers in a marriage, there is not time for a two-person career. A woman in museum administration stated:

> Lots of people here wonder whether I really am married, because Charlie doesn't come to all the events involved in what I do. I guess you could call those the traditional functions that a spouse does for a career. But Charlie contributes in the ways that I consider valuable—he provides support.

Several men commented on the trade-offs of having a career wife as opposed to a corporate wife. In general, men and women alike tended to feel that, in the current era, marriage to an independently successful spouse was probably more help than hindrance. A businessman in his early 40s stated:

> As a young man, it probably would have helped to present a corporate wife. But she didn't want to do that. It probably didn't make a lot of difference. Now she can only help—people say, he's married to an interesting and successful woman, so he must be interesting.

Although many participants discussed how they and their spouses did not perform these traditional duties for each other's careers, none of the husbands or wives reported that the lack of a two-person career actually impeded his or her career development.

Scheduling. Approximately one quarter of men and women indicated that the spouse's scheduling demands and conflicts, including out-of-town travel, hurt their careers. Frequently, one spouse's career was characterized by greater inflexibility in and lack of control over work schedule. As a result, the other person felt compelled to constantly bend his or her more flexible schedule to accommodate family tasks.

Geography

In the life of the dual-career couple, geography often becomes a pivotal issue. Two thirds of the participants mentioned geography as a way in which the spouses had facilitated or impeded their career. Moving for the other person's career can be appreciated as a contribution to its development; at the same time, it may represent some sacrifice in terms of one's own career. Decisions *not* to move are as crucial to examine within this context as decisions *to* move.

For many couples, the question of when and where to move forms a *leitmotif* that runs through the years. A man in his early 30s stated:

> The perennial conflict of the two-career family, which we are always discussing, is where we should locate. It's a very difficult problem when both people are advancing up the ladder. We will both make compromises. We will not get an optimal solution, but hopefully a satisfactory one.

The ideal, of course, is to find a location that can facilitate both careers; the reality is that compromise is probable. A man in his early 40s, poised on the brink of a career change, articulated the trade-offs that contribute to his dilemma:

> What's so hard about where we are right now is that we're in a place where her career will suffer if we move, or my career will suffer if we don't, or our personal life will suffer, if I get a job out of town and commute.

There were a number of dimensions pertaining to geographic moves along which the couples varied. Some careers require little mobility: Once established somewhere, the likelihood of a move is minimal or even nil. Professionals in private practice (physicians, dentists, lawyers, and mental health professionals) are representative of this category, as are tenured faculty in some fields. On the other hand, these professions make it highly difficult to move if the spouse's career dictates. At the other end of the continuum are positions where necessary moves are practically guaranteed: many corporate positions, junior faculty at competitive universities, and postdoctoral positions.

In many instances, the measure of whether a decision about a move proved benefical or detrimental to a career only emerges many years down the road. In the case of one couple, for example, the wife was offered an excellent opportunity in another city, and they decided to move when the husband located a position comparable to his current one in the new location. However, several years later the husband found himself with no promotion opportunities, whereas he was certain that he would have advanced in his prior place of employment.

For many couples, the decision-making process around geographic moves reflects in essence how the two careers are viewed and valued within the family. In particular, the importance of the woman's career is sometimes most challenged or affirmed around this issue.

In nearly half of the couples, all decisions to move or stay to date had been based on the husband's career. In only a couple of families had all decisions about geographical location been dictated by the wife's career. Both husband's and wife's careers had influenced the geographical decisions of approximately one third of the couples (i.e., a decision was based equally on husband's and wife's careers, or one move had been dictated by husband's career and another move by wife's career). For a few couples, no moves had been prompted by career factors.

When the couple subscribes to the traditional expectation that the husband's career is more salient than the wife's, moving for his career is often an unquestioned assumption. Women merely follow along, and frequently do not begin to look seriously into work possibilities until after the move is in progress or completed. A woman in her early 40s described a move early in their marriage:

> The move here certainly wasn't researched well or explored fully. He was given an opportunity for work, and it seemed good. That's how we do things: We take advantage of being in the right place at the right time, and letting things happen as they will. [Did you think of the consequences for your career?] No, I figured I could find work, so it didn't seem an issue.

Jane, a social scientist in her mid-30s currently on a postdoctoral fellowship, said her husband's career should dictate their moves, due to his greater income:

> I think when we get to the next juncture, it's more likely that we'll go where George wants to, because he has greater earning potential. So we would have to make decisions that are best for him. I mean, I love my work—and want to keep growing in it. But you have to think about the economic return, too.

This seemingly pragmatic perspective reflects many of the contradictions and complexities inherent to this transitional era. Jane stated at another point during the interview that she perceived it as problematic that women tend to gravitate toward lower paying positions than men and are less successful at demanding more money. Hence, Jane recognized that women tend to occupy lower paying positions but also felt that her lower pay made it reasonable for her to follow rather than lead geographic moves of her family.

It is expected that a move organized around the husband's career often hampers the woman's career progress. A vicious cycle is thus established: Women begin in lower paying jobs and are likely to remain there because they feel they should not make moves for their career that they would make for their husband's career. Beyond the economic issues may lie other feelings about directing geographic moves on behalf of one's own career. Jane wondered aloud what would happen if she were the higher earning spouse:

> If I earned more, I don't know, because I think work is more important to a man than it is to a woman. So if he got a great job across the country I would probably go. I think what he was getting would matter to him more than what I would be giving up would matter to me.

Again, the issue of differential career salience is key.

In many couples, however, the traditional expectation of the man's career dictating the family's location and relocation has been challenged. A consideration of geographic moves in the life of the couple needs to adopt a dynamic perspective: When expectations have changed over time, negotiation of geographic moves has also evolved. A man in his early 40s described this evolution:

> I think we began our marriage with a traditional, unexamined sense that my career was going to be the dominant career, so we would make sacrifices for that and that she would be supportive of that. It was a sense that when I decided to relocate to go to grad school—well, we talked a bit about what that would mean for her work, but it wasn't the kind of equal dealing and trading as six years later when we talked about where she would locate her career. During that time, there was not only a flowering of her career, but also a growing awareness that she ought to have a robust career as well, which was tied into feminism, and an idea that we should have a more equal kind of relationship.

In order to ensure equality in decision making about geographic location, several couples had devised explicit formulas to guide the process. For example, some agreed that they would alternate who could make the decision to move; some had devised an equation for what constituted a desirable move. One couple, for example, agreed that each spouse had to feel that the move was a step up in order for it to be viewed as worthwhile, and they alternated who had final say in the decision. In reality, these guidelines tended to be bent and adapted to the particular situation, but they provided a sense of control over an otherwise anxiety-producing, unpredictable situation. In addition, these formulas represented an explicit counterexpectation to the traditional assumption of male career as primary.

Some couples said they would weigh their careers equally in decisions about moves but had not yet tested their resolve. Geographic moves are interwoven with many other issues pertaining to the equality of the two careers in the life of the dual-career couple. One man explained that he feels safe proclaiming that they would move were his wife to receive a certain kind of job offer, because it is apparent that she is not investing the energy and ambition into her career that would make that offer a probability:

> If Sue got offered a fabulous job, I would move. I believe that this is very important; what's fair is fair. Of course, I'm talking from a safe position, because Sue isn't as career-oriented as I am, and I don't think she would ever be offered that kind of job. She's not on that track.

Commuting. The question of geography does not only provoke the question of whether to move or not to move. It also raises the specter of another increasing possibility: whether or not to commute. The definition of commuting has expanded. Working one place and living elsewhere is not a new addition to the work-family system: Many of the dual-career spouses' fathers lived in suburban towns and then commuted to urban work settings. But the concept of having two separate residences and, typically, living independently for portions of each week is a commuting arrangement born of the dual-career marriage.[11] Even spouses who had not yet had any periods of being a *commuter marriage* recognized it as an option and spontaneously discussed its viability for them. A woman who interrupted her graduate education to move with her husband to his new job explained: "I could have stayed in school and commuted to see my husband. That didn't appeal to me. I decided instead to move with him, and work while he went to school." One man wondered aloud whether he and his wife might try a phase of commuting at some point in the future but felt that there were limits to the geographic distance that would be workable:

> When my firm recently opened a San Francisco office, that posed a lot of challenges to people. One guy had the company agree to fly him back every second weekend to see his wife and kids; another had his wife look for work out there, and they ended up relocating. I might have been willing to try the second option; I would not have done the first.

One quarter of the couples had commuted for at least one year. For a couple of families, this arrangement represents a long-term solution

---

[11]For a full discussion of commuter marriage, see Gerstel and Gross (1984).

to careers being located in separate cities; for several other couples, a commuting arrangement was temporary. The three quarters of the couples who had not commuted tended to describe it as a last resort option, and many saw it as an impossible solution. However, the spouses who had commuted tended to have at least some, and often many, positive responses to it. They described that the commuting arrangement facilitated compartmentalization of work and family and long stretches of uninterrupted work time. A man who had for several years spent weekends with his wife and lived apart from her the remainder of the week stated: "I considered it as close to ideal as I've ever gotten. I could work very hard all week without limits, and then punctuate the work week with weekends of being together and romantic."

However, disadvantages also were discussed. When commuting couples have children, the arrangement is clearly more complicated for the spouse who serves as a single parent for a portion of each week. A man in a long-term commuting marriage noted:

> Living apart might seem a big disadvantage, but it is also healthy and positive. It means I can work in the office as late as I want, without worrying about coming home to see my son, and he doesn't lie there wondering why his father hasn't come home before he goes to bed. He may wonder about that anyway—but as soon as he's old enough, he'll understand that it's because we're pursuing different careers. It's nice then to have the time to sit down, do our taxes, read a book. This is my side of it, not hers, since she has our child with her. From my point of view, it's been healthy for our marriage.

His wife qualified her endorsement of the arrangement, agreeing that it is far less optimal now that they have a child:

> Before we had a son, I liked having the two places. I would take care of all my work up there, and then do my personal life things here. I liked it being compartmentalized. Now, with a child, things are more difficult and complicated.

The descriptions of the commuting lifestyle bring to mind another modern group of dual-residence citizens: children of joint custody. The challenges of having two homes, two sets of friends, and a constant re-acclimation to one's environment are considerable. A man who had used a commuting arrangement with his wife many years earlier and was now considering it again reflected:

> It wasn't great, and I don't relish it happening again, which it may. I found it disconcerting to have two lives, with two separate sets of relationships.

It was hard to keep her apprised of what was happening in my life here. Also, she had the child, so she had to cope with arranging all the child care and all, in addition to our physical separation.

Couples tended to focus on the advantages and difficulties of the commuting arrangement in terms of concrete, pragmatic details. In addition, however, living apart half the week would seem to pose considerable challenges to the emotional continuity of a marriage and to usual expectations for and habits of intimacy. A man who relocated for a job, while his wife remained to complete her graduate education, commented on these issues:

We also miss each other when we're apart. But maybe it has to do with our socialization: We end up coping with pragmatics, not our feelings. I think we both put protective layers around our feelings. We insulate them in an effort to effectively take care of child care and cooking.

His wife described the complex feelings stimulated by their period of commuting:

There was a feeling of desertion. We had finally gotten us all in one city, and settled, and then he got the job. It wasn't his fault, but that doesn't mean you don't have feelings. I like having him around; it was hard psychologically. We became somewhat distanced from each other. Also, during that time we decided to have another child, and then I didn't get pregnant for a long time. So things hadn't been completed yet—and when things get taken away from a not complete picture, the incompleteness is felt even more.

It appears that, for some dual-career couples, commuting may solve the dilemma of careers literally pulling the family in two different directions. However, the majority of the dual-career couples in the sample found commuting unacceptable. For all the couples, issues of where to live remain complex and often difficult.

Talking About Work

Talking about work with the spouse plays a significant role in the life of the dual-career couple. Of the time that couples spent talking together, they estimated that an average of half that time was devoted to talk about work. Given this focus on each other's career, it is not surprising that spouses appeared to know a great deal about each other's work lives.

Talking about work with the spouse serves a number of functions.

Because couples spend many hours apart each week while working, talking about what transpired during those many hours becomes a primary means of staying connected. Talk about work serves as emotional glue between the separate work worlds inhabited by the spouses and provides a possible means of achieving and maintaining intimacy in the face of daily separation and autonomous work lives. At another level, many people rely on discussing the day's events in order to move beyond them. Whether in play-by-play or general summary form, discussion of the recent happenings provides closure to the work day and eases transition into the family and home environment.

Gender Differences in Work Talk.   Interestingly, the spouses' talk about careers is asymmetrical: Couples appear to devote more airtime to discussing the woman's career than the man's. Half the men and women reported that the couple talked about the wife's career an average of twice as much as they did about the husband's career. One third felt they spoke about the two careers equally, and a few spouses said the man's career received more time.

How did couples interpret this gender difference? Many participants attributed it to differences in personality or personal style. The difference sometimes was explained by an emphasis on the man, such as his being less inclined to talk about work. A woman stated: "I'd like him to tell me more about his work than he does. He's the type of person who, when he comes home from the office, he doesn't want to think about it." Alternatively, the difference was attributed to the wife, such as her greater need to discuss things, as one woman commented:

> We have very different thresholds regarding how urgent it is to talk about work. I have a lower threshold, so I usually start talking about my work first. I have more need to get it out, whereas he can wait, and then talk about it or not, depending.

Typically, the press to talk is related to emotionally laden material. One woman described:

> I think I use talk more as an emotional outlet. So I'll talk angrily, let off steam. John lets off steam too, but he does it in different ways. He'll be moody and dark when things aren't going well at work, but he may not explode about them externally. I'll be more tempestuous.

Ron said that he avoided telling his wife, Kristin, the details of his work problems in order "to spare her." Kristin's view was that she would prefer to be told:

When something big happens at work, I feel I have to get it off my chest, whereas Ron can't do that. And I think that has to do with why I'm up here asleep and he's still downstairs at midnight, mulling things over from the day. I think it would be good for him to talk about it.

Spouses also said the type of work that each performed affected how much they could discuss work. People argued, for example, that some work did not lend itself to discussion with the spouse because of its technical or confidential nature. However, these attributions, although plausible when taken on an individual basis, were not consistent across couples. One couple, for example, extensively discussed the wife's work as a psychotherapist, viewing it as work "about people" and therefore intuitively comprehensible to the non-therapist husband. In another couple, the husband's work as a therapist was rarely talked about because it was viewed as "*just* about people" and therefore less exciting than the wife's work as a corporate lawyer. In another instance, a couple felt that they talked more about her work because it tended to be continuous over time and therefore made an unfolding, developing story. Her husband's work, in contrast, changed frequently and they described it as too hard to keep up with. For another couple, the exact opposite occurred, as the husband described:

> My work is long, sustained projects that span a number of years. To talk about it frequently would be repetitive, whereas Joyce does work that is more changing, choppy, so that more is new more frequently. So we talk about hers a lot more, since it's more novel and exciting.

Hence, although couples understood their disproportionate talk about their work to be related to the *kind* of work that each did, no consistent patterns emerged about kinds of work that tended to be talked about more. Rather, the difference appears to be related to gender, although couples rarely recognized it as such.

Regardless of the *kinds* of work that men and women were engaged in, the *ways* in which they discussed their jobs related to gender. In general, the spouses reported that women focused more on experiential aspects and exploration of options of a work situation and men more on technical issues and concrete solutions. These differences sometimes enabled complementary, mutually helpful exchanges, as a woman stated:

> We're very different. I want to know the feeling of a person: How did they look, talk, sit, and what did they feel like to you. Dan is much more into telling me, "Now, you've got to write that memo," because those are the

things I don't naturally do. And what I point out to him, he doesn't usually think of.

However, the differences in style and focus also produced tension and frustration, as a man described:

My view of what constitutes working through a problem in terms of resolving any emotional difficulties probably differs very substantially from hers. I need to talk about something less, and/or have a better ability to suppress it than she does. She needs to work it through more than I do. There have been many times when she's said that I'm not being supportive enough, and I feel I'm at my wits' end and that we've talked about it up the wazoo. So it's a different perception of how much talk or how many times is enough.

His wife corroborated and expanded on this view:

This is a perpetual source of argument. If I have a nasty problem situation which I lay out, Glen jumps right to the solution. It may be fatigue on his part; it could be lots of reasons. But he is very uncomfortable with too much tension or complaining. I often want someone to help me define the problem, but he'll get irritated and say, "Well, why don't you do this?"

The picture that emerges is that women wish to explore interpersonal and emotional dimensions of a work situation and that men tend to problem solve and offer advice. Each gender articulated some appreciation for the other's style: Men expressed gratitude for their wives' input on work relationships and "delicate matters in the office" (as one man put it), and women felt their husbands provided helpful advice and concrete suggestions. Frequently, however, men and women expressed discontent with the spouse's input and a preference for their own way of discussing work. One man commented:

I see myself as a slightly better listener. [How so?] Maybe it's that I'm a better advice giver. Maybe it's that I'm a man, and therefore slightly more detached from the problems a woman encounters.

Changes in Work Talk Over Time. It is important to note that a couple's talk about work shifts in quantity and quality over time. A man stated: "I think we have a family mind, which sometimes focuses on her work for a time, sometimes on mine, and then sometimes on something like canoeing. We go through stages." One variable that influenced the balance of talk about work for most couples was one person's career being in a state of transition or crisis. In general, a developmental juncture in a career attracts the joint attention of the dual-career spouses. A woman stated:

> One situation that triggers thoughtful reflective discussions is when one person is clearly at a transitional point, and the family as well as the person is therefore in a state of flux. To the extent possible, you try to sort out options, pros and cons. Two years ago that was me; recently it's been him.

Spouses tended to adjust how they spoke about their own career when the spouse was encountering difficulty. If one person's career was in jeopardy or at a standstill, the other spouse generally approached discussions about work with care and caution. One woman reported:

> When he's feeling insecure about his career, he tends to withdraw from talking about it. He feels that I can be critical; I'm not sure whether it's that or that he's sensitive. I consciously walk on eggshells at those times, because he needs no more blows.

Participants often recognized the fact and degree to which they had adjusted their own talk about work depending on the spouse's relative happiness or success on the job. For many, this calibration was deliberate and important, as one woman described:

> I think I've gauged that really closely. There have been periods in the not-too-distant past where I was very careful of what I said, and how it came out, because I thought it might have an impact that we really didn't need. Such as talking about salary increases that otherwise I'd be ecstatic about, but instead would just report and that would be that. Or if he was having a hard time with the boss, and so was I, I'd limit how much bitching I'd do. I'm not sure how effective I was, but I was certainly very conscious of it.

Many participants commented that they were considering for the first time during the interview whether their spouses made similar adjustments in work talk. A woman noted:

> Hmm, well, my hunch is that during that period when I felt so bad about my career, he downplayed some of his triumphs. It was diplomatic on his part. I know I did that when he was an intern and so tired. I discussed career issues with a good friend, and just gave him a snapshot of what was going on.

COMPARISON AND COMPETITION

Parsons (1942) contended that the competition for status that would emerge from husband and wife both working would spell the demise of marriage. Issues of comparison and competition were predicted to be among the most complex dynamics with which to contend in the dual-career marriage. In the traditional marriage, there is little overlap of roles or turf: The work world is allocated to the man and the home is assigned to the woman. In the dual-career marriage, men and women straddle both worlds. The work world in particular, with its emphasis on success and achievement and its many barometers of progress (promotions, salary, prestige), provides ample opportunity for comparison and competition between spouses.

Feelings of competition between spouses in the dual-career marriage are complicated for a number of reasons. Most people believe that although competition may be acceptable and even condoned in the work world, the family is a different matter. For men more than women, competition seems socially sanctioned, but neither gender has a norm of cross-gender competition. Hence, spouses typically said that, in the ideal marriage, there are no feelings of competition between spouses. How, then, are such feelings tolerated, admitted, and dealt with in a healthy, nondestructive way?

The Presence of Competitive Feelings

Competition is most likely to be evident in the dual-career couple during times when at least one spouse is feeling insecure, anxious, or frustrated in his or her career. This situation obtained for approximately two thirds of the couples at least temporarily. Dynamics of comparison and competition may be present at other times as well, but when both spouses feel satisfied with and successful in their jobs, these issues appear to be relatively benign and unobtrusive.

Different factors appear to foster feelings of competition between spouses. One is differential career standing, where one spouse enters the career track well behind the other. For example, a woman entered her field many years after her husband was already established, which proved a constant source of frustration and set the stage for her "trying always to catch up." This situation resembles sibling rivalry, in which the older sibling retains the seemingly unfair advantage of having started ahead. Alternatively, spouses may begin their careers synchronously, but one person's career then progresses more rapidly through the ranks. One husband and wife graduated from college and simultaneously began their careers; when she received several promotions that were unmatched in his career, he began to struggle with intense feelings of comparison and competition. Another factor is when one spouse feels unacknowledged or frustrated in his or her career. One man found himself frustrated by a field that offered few possibilities for promotion or recognition, whereas his wife's career accelerated dramatically and received public acknowledgment.

The competitive dynamics typically emerge as most salient in the person whose career is less well established, secure, or successful. As one man summarized:

> I guess I don't worry about the competitive thing because maybe I think I would win that competition. The question of competition seems interdependent with the question of who is going to win that competition. If you're going to win, it doesn't seem as significant.

For some, feelings of comparison and competition contributed to concrete changes in career. One man said of his decision to return to school for a higher level degree: "Probably some of it was to stay abreast of her." The spouse may provide a barometer of progress against which to measure oneself. A businessman whose wife is also in business stated: "When she started to advance, I started to think, am I ever going to make it?" These feelings can be hard to acknowledge and to work through. A man who struggled with difficult feelings in response to his wife reaping higher pay increases and promotions commented: "She had the feeling that she hadn't done anything wrong. And she hadn't. [Did you feel that she had?] Yes, sometimes."

Because competitive feelings toward the spouse were viewed as largely inappropriate, it is not surprising that efforts at denial and avoidance were frequent. A woman described her lack of patience and tolerance for her husband's competitive feelings toward her:

> He felt a competition that I didn't feel. [How did you deal with that?] Mostly I didn't think it was right, that it was an incorrect assessment of the situation, that we shouldn't be competitive, that you couldn't compare. So mostly I didn't pay attention to it. We talked about it after the fact, but not very much. So I know there were times that it was an undercurrent for him. I do remember, on occasion, being frustrated that he felt it as much as he did.

Some people employed explicit strategies to try to minimize competition, such as detaching themselves from the spouse's work. A woman described:

I think I'm not as interested in what he's doing because—that's my competition—I feel like if I read his grant proposal, then I'll feel like I should do more myself. But this isn't a question of limited resources, and I don't think wanting to outperform him is a motive. I think it has to do more with envy, jealousy—wanting it for me. But since we're both doing well and getting established in our careers, it's okay.

With energy directed toward reducing the presence and visibility of competitive feelings, it is sometimes unclear where these feelings go. A woman in her upper-30s stated:

I compare myself to him mostly when I feel badly about what I'm doing. Like I envy his being able to write so freely and easily, especially when I'm trying to write something. But it tends to go underground. I have the feeling that it may be more there, but I'm not sure what happens to it.

Straightforward discussion of feelings of competition rarely occurred between spouses. In the words of one woman, "head-on collisions" on the subject were relatively rare. However, dynamics of comparison and competition carry great potential to produce tension and conflict. One woman described an earlier period of her marriage:

When I first got out of graduate school, I realized that I had made a mistake. I wasn't in the right field for me. His career was sailing, soaring. That contrast was hard to deal with. I know this put a lot of stress on the marriage. We fought a lot then, and now we rarely do.

Some spouses were aware that feelings of competition that were generally inaccessible for direct discussion were displaced frequently onto other issues that provided a more concrete, less taboo battleground for discussion and argument. Most common were debates over allocation of time for career versus time for domestic tasks. A man in his early 40s, who described struggling with feelings of competition towards his highly successful wife, reported:

We discuss these issues indirectly. Mostly through talking and arguing about other things—like work schedules, vacation schedules, who stays home when somebody has the measles, who owes whom what favor around the house.

A woman in her early 40s described:

> I think the main area of competition for us is who is going to have more opportunity to be successful—as in, time to do their work. There is a bit of jockeying for that, which is fairly upfront.

Themes of allocation of time and division of chores are not merely concrete and significant issues for daily living in the dual-career marriage. They also serve as receptacles for displaced feelings about more ambiguous, complex, or taboo subjects such as comparison and competition.

The reverse kind of competition also occurs, in which each spouse strives to demonstrate that he or she is contributing a fair share to the household chores and *not* claiming too much time for career. A woman described:

> The main thing we compete in, tit for tat, is with the children. It's a sort of one-upmanship, a question of who has done more. I know there are times when Lou will rush home and say, "You didn't make the lunches, did you?" and I'll say, "Yes, I did." I know in his mind he was sort of hoping he could make them, because that's a point for him. Or he'll say a week in advance, "You know, Wednesday I'm going to be taking the kids to school" and he'll want me to register that all week. (laugh)

At a basic level, success of dual-career spouses is not based on a hydraulic model: An increase in one spouse's career success does not necessarily diminish success for the other. Many spouses argued that they do not compete with each other because they are not working for limited resources. However, a broader view of the work-family system suggests that there may be some contingency between the success of the two careers. In the dual-career marriage, the balance between time and success is often highly delicate. A man in his mid-30s commented:

> If I were more successful because Liz felt I took advantage of her and our relationship, then she would be pissed. If she were more successful because she dumped things on me, that would be a problem too.

To some extent, then, there *are* limited resources. When one spouse's success entails devotion of more time to career and less time to domestic work, the other spouse's increased domestic work may translate into diminished success.

Factors Mitigating Against Competition

Nearly half the men and women contended that competition and comparison have not been issues in their marriage. Most frequently, they attributed this to differences in their careers: "You can't compare them because they're apples and oranges." These differences were sometimes deliberate, such as when a woman told her husband not to consider her field when he was contemplating a job change. For the majority of spouses, these differences were more coincidental but much appreciated. Typical was a man who commented: "I think it would be really hard if we were in the same field. This way, we each have our separate thing, so that we don't have a need or a chance to compare much." Even spouses in the same field often considered themselves to be different because of their distinct subspecialties. Other couples claimed comparison to be difficult because of different markers of success. A man commented: "It's easy to stay vague about who is ahead because our careers are more amorphous and less hierarchical than some fields, like business for example."

However, the reasons people gave for the lack of competition between spouses were inconsistent across couples. In contrast to the man just cited, one woman perceived the comparability of her husband's and her own job rank as protective against competition:

It's great for us that we're both in kind of similar positions within our companies. We do totally different things, but since we're both middle management, we have a lot to talk about. And this way we don't feel competitive, because we're kind of the same.

Some argued that synchrony of career development works against competitive dynamics, as a woman reported: "I think maybe we're not competitive because we just started out together, first as students, and since then both of us have evolved." However, others felt that different ranks reduced competition, as a woman stated: "He's always been so much more advanced than me, so it would be presumptuous and kind of silly to compete. I think it would be much harder if we were at the same point in our careers." Some spouses contended that having two careers decreased problematic competition. They argued that each spouse is doing what she or he wants to, and therefore is less likely to feel competitive toward the other. A woman lawyer said she saw greater potential for competition in the traditional one-career marriage:

I think this way we have a more balanced relationship, less competition. If I had given up a career, or chosen a less time-consuming or stressful field for the sake of time commitment alone, there might have been more jealousy or resentment. It probably would have manifested itself very subtly, but it would have been there, and at some point wreaked havoc on the relationship.

It seems possible that couples wanted very much to avoid feelings of competition and therefore have created plausible reasons why they do not experience such feelings. The inconsistency of these reasons across couples suggests that the reasons may pertain little to the relative presence or absence of competition. The factor that appears most salient as a buffer against divisive competition is the genuine desire for the spouse to do well and to be happy, a desire that comes most naturally when one is feeling successful and happy oneself. The other's career success is viewed as increasing the family's happiness; the couple is viewed as a partnership to which each spouse contributes his or her degree of job satisfaction, feelings of self-esteem and self-fulfillment, and income. Success is desired for each spouse in order to increase the joint level of job satisfaction and, hence, marital and life satisfaction. Many people also conveyed that a spouse's career success is desirable because it permits them to do well in their own careers without creating friction or an imbalance. When both spouses are doing well and feel confident about their careers, they are most likely to applaud and enjoy the spouse's successes.

Comparative Success

The overwhelming majority of spouses desired success for their spouses as they did for themselves: The consensus is that married life with a content, successful, self-confident spouse is far more pleasant than with someone who is insecure, struggling, and unhappy. But what if spouses do not achieve equivalent success? Would it be easier if a discrepancy in success favored the husband's career or the wife's? When asked this question, participants responded with hesitation. Often, they asked for the question to be repeated, or they began to wander off on a tangent before coming back and asking, "Now wait, what was the question again?"

The results suggest a pocket of enduring tradition. Almost all the women felt it would be easier for their career to be less successful than their husband's career than for the reverse to be true; the remaining few felt that it would be equally hard either way. This was often admitted with reluctance ("Even though I like to think we've moved beyond this, I have to admit . . .") and shame ("I'm embarrassed to say this, but . . ."). A woman in her mid-30s said after a long pause: "I think, yes, I think it's true: I would rather he be more successful than me. I hate to admit it. I wish it weren't so. But unfortunately I think it is." Many women qualified their responses with references to societal attitudes: "Well, given the sexist world we live in. . . ." or "It would be harder for him because of what other people would say." A lawyer in her early 30s explained:

> I wouldn't have the same social pressures from the community and people in the field. People would say, "So, she can't make it in law, so what—she's got her kids. Maybe when they're grown up, she'll pick something else up. Not a big deal." That would make the situation worse for me, of course. But if it happened to Stuart, people would say, "Oh, poor Stuart. His wife is the one who is doing this to him. She's making him help at home, so he doesn't have time to work."

Some women reasoned that because comparative success did not matter to them and might to their husbands, his career might as well surpass hers. A woman in her mid-30s reported:

> I don't think it would make a difference to me, as long as I felt good about what I was doing. If one career were going to be more important, since it makes no difference to me, then probably it should be his. I'm not sure that he wouldn't feel better psychologically if it were his career that were more important.

The assessment of the comparative success issue tended to focus on the husband's feelings and to revolve around the greater importance of work to his sense of self than to hers. Most women contended that a foundering career would incur a greater injury to the male ego than it would to the female's. A woman in her mid-30s reported: "I think his self-definition is much more dependent than mine on his career. So if his career weren't going well, I'd feel terribly worried about him." A few women said they would feel guilty about their own career's success if their husband's career encountered difficulty.

For many women, their own career provides a minimum standard against which the husband's career is assessed: The implication is that his career should be *at least* as successful as hers. A woman in her upper-30s described:

> If his career were less successful than mine, it would make me nervous. I would wonder, what's stopping him, what's holding him up. I think maybe it has to do with being a woman. I need him to be successful.

Some women recognized the underlying traditional expectations that the man be successful in his career. If the woman is *also* successful, that is fine; but if she is successful *instead* of the man, that threatens a basic, deeply ingrained assumption. A woman in her mid-30s described her responses to a period in which her husband's career encountered difficulty:

> It's easier for him to cope with my feeling weak about and having problems with my career than it is for me to cope with him feeling weak. It must be sex-linked. I could deal fine with him being upset because of other things, but his employment failure was very threatening to me. [Do you have a sense what was threatening about it?] I think it goes way back. I was brought up as a little girl who was dependent. I don't want to belittle what I do, but I was brought up to be protected and cared for. So even though I know I can take care of myself, here he was, looking like maybe he wasn't going to be able to provide, and I didn't like that.

Many women acknowledged the cultural tradition underlying their preference for his career to be more successful. This question of comparative success, as much as any other in the interview, brought these underlying traditional expectations to the fore. A woman in her mid-30s exclaimed:

> I guess what this shows is that I'm enculturated! It wouldn't be a problem at all for me if his career were more successful. I expect to be successful personally, but the fact that I have a baby and I'm doing well at work, I almost see that as a measure of success, keeping everything going. Whereas men are from an early age expected to go to work. So maybe what I'm saying is that it has to do with the male ego, and that it's easier for a woman to have a husband who is very successful than vice versa.

Approximately half the men reported that it would be easier for their wife's career to be less successful than for their career to be the less successful one. Many men admitted this only reluctantly, much as their wives had. Many men explained it in terms of external factors:

> I think as a couple we would have less anxiety if her career foundered than if mine did. I think it relates to the income differential. I don't think it's a value judgment about my career being more valuable, but just our functioning as a unit. We're both invested in our careers. [Is that symmetrical?] Well, actually I think she's probably more invested in my career than I am in hers.

Other men, like this man in his early 40s, were very direct in their replies:

> It's easier if the male is more successful. [Easier for whom?] For both. My job is my identity more than it is for a woman. For a woman, if she's

unsuccessful with her job, she could be successful in her other job, as a mother and taking care of the house and being an emotional provider.

The other half of the men resembled the few women who felt that an imbalance of success in either direction would be equally difficult. No man or woman in the sample felt that it would be easier if the woman's career were more successful than the man's.

Men wondered aloud about the possible consequences of having the wife's career become more successful. A few spontaneously proclaimed things like, "Well, if you're wondering whether it would lead to divorce or something, no," implying that the potential consequences were quite serious. Some talked about the challenge it would pose. For many couples, it would represent a further and significant extension of nontraditional reality. A man in his upper-30s stated:

I would need to learn to live with it. I don't have any older role models where the wife's career is more successful. Even though all of the women of my generation in my family have careers, in every case the man's career is still the more successful one.

A few expressed concern about the consequences, like a man in his mid-30s:

I would like to think I would handle it well, but I don't know. I would be happy for her, but you never know. I know a couple that had the same field, and her career really took off and his stayed the same. And they eventually got divorced. So I don't know how it would work out.

Most explicit was a man whose career had lagged behind his wife's for a period earlier in the marriage:

I can imagine it happening, that her career were much more successful. It would be hard for me to adjust to. I think the consequences would be dire. [Such as?] Such as marital separation. [Can you say what would make it so difficult?] I think that, well, a large amount of my pride would prevent me from dealing with it very effectively.

Given the number of couples who considered it preferable for an imbalance to favor his career rather than hers, do couples contain and try to avoid competitive dynamics by cooperatively creating this situation? One man asserted: "We're very competitive people, but I don't compete with my wife. I enjoy competing and I enjoy winning. I don't want to be second best." Would he feel competitive with his wife if his career were second best to hers? His career is, according to objective markers and to both spouses' accounts, significantly farther along than hers. A crucial factor was that the couple followed the common pattern described earlier of his graduate education pre-ceeding hers. He therefore became established much earlier than she.

Two Careers in the Same Field

The most frequent explanation that spouses offered for why they did not feel competitive with each other was that they do different things. What happens when spouses do the same thing? In about one third of the couples, husband and wife were in the same field. It is certainly common for spouses to meet through common interests, in graduate school or in the workplace. If anything, with trends toward delayed marriage among professionals, it might be expected that fewer people would meet their prospective spouse and marry in college and that more people would marry in graduate school or after entering the work world. This shift may increase the likelihood of spouses meeting due to overlap in career interests.

Typically, the spouses whose careers were in different fields imag-ined that it would be far more difficult to have careers in the same field. However, dual-career spouses who shared a field described many more benefits than the dual-career couples in different fields imagined. Spouses in the same field spoke frequently of the tremendous support and understanding that a fellow insider can provide. A man in invest-ment banking described:

> Many nights you just don't get home, and that's not counting the 120 days I was on the road last year. I would call Sue to say I was about to leave the office, and then 15 minutes later call to say I'd probably be there all night. If Sue had never been exposed to the unpredictability and the incredibility of that work schedule, it would have produced great strains. But instead, here she was doing the same kind of things, with many all-night sessions herself. If she'd been a teacher, like the wife of a friend of mine, that would have been a problem. They got a divorce.

Rather than viewing it primarily as a disadvantage to be in the same field, almost all spouses perceived their shared field to be an advan-tage. Some found it hard to imagine being married to someone in a different field, as a woman social worker stated:

> I think it might be difficult to be involved with someone not in the mental health field. Unless it were someone who had been in therapy. I think it

must seem so bizarre. It would be very strange not to be able to communicate about psychotherapy.

At the same time, certain comparisons appear to be potentiated by similar careers. The requisite skills and talents and the system of rewards, honors, and promotions become highly similar or even identical when spouses are in the same field. Some comparison and competition becomes probable and may become a challenge to manage effectively. For example, a couple in the same academic field struggled with two illustrative issues: junior-senior status differences between wife and husband, and complex turf issues that arise from continuous dialogue about work ideas over the years:

He: When we first thought about getting married, I thought, that's ridiculous, because we're in the same field. Of course, we did it anyway. If she were, say, a lawyer, I'd learn a lot about law, and there'd be fewer turf problems. But I don't know. We share a lot of intellectual excitement, which is a lot of fun. We think totally differently, even though we have a similar professional background. So it allows me to see things through someone's eyes who I trust and feel comfortable with, but who thinks quite differently. So I never would have predicted this or recommended it, but it's been good. I could see for some people, they would see each other all day at work, and then come home—it would be too much. But for us, we don't see each other enough. We'll plan lunch together, just to get to talk about professional things. So it has worked really well for us.

She: I don't think I would have chosen it this way, but it's great to have your husband in the same discipline, as long as you're not competing. You have a lot of common interests, you both know the issues, it's very exciting and stimulating. You can come home and complain, and the other person knows exactly what you're talking about. Only problem is that because we talk to each other so much, it's sometimes hard to say whose idea is whose. So then we have to sit down and fight it out. That's a problem with all colleagues, but working it out with your husband is different. Plus, the person who is more junior, who is me in this case, has to keep saying to herself, "You can't get caught up in this." I'll say, "How come no one's inviting me to any international meetings, and they're inviting you," and he'll say, "When I was at your level, I got invited to one or two meetings a year, just like you are." So it's a matter of getting used to being constantly exposed to another person who gets more glory.

The same-field, dual-career marriage highlights some of both the advantages and disadvantages of dual-career marriage in general. The benefits derive from understanding each other's work and from the comraderie that comes from shared professional interests. The costs stem from the fertile ground for issues of comparison and competition.

THE DUAL-INCOME MARRIAGE

One of the obvious yet profound differences between a one-career marriage and the dual-career marriage is the contribution of both dual-career spouses to the family's financial resources. This simple fact carries many not-so-simple implications for marital and family life. Income intersects with issues of comparison and competition, division of labor, power dynamics, and perspectives on women's careers.

Income and Comparison

Across careers that may differ widely in honors, awards, and promotions, money often serves as a common denominator for comparison. The man earns more than the woman in approximately half of the couples in the sample. For these couples, the wife's income represents a significant departure from the traditional marriage in which the husband was a solo breadwinner. However, his provision of the dominant share of the family's income preserves a relative balance of tradition and often reinforces a sense of his career as more salient.

For the other half of the couples, the dimension of income has more of a nontraditional cast. In about one quarter of the couples, husband and wife earn comparable incomes (within $4,000 of each other), whereas in another quarter the wife earns more than the husband.

What meaning does this issue of relative income carry for couples? Some couples profess it to be relatively trivial. Often, they approach income highly pragmatically, considering only how much money their combined incomes provide. One man, for example, had chosen his career largely because it paid well. He answered questions about career choice with responses like "A career was always assumed because you had to earn a living" and "This line of work seemed practical and feasible. I knew I could support a family with it." One apparent outcome of his approach is that money seems more pragmatic than symbolic. He and his wife earn nearly identical (and sizable) salaries, and both believe that additional income is appreciated, from whichever source it comes. These couples often employed the language of a partnership in discussing income.

For other couples, income provides fertile ground for comparison and competition. The gap between many husbands' and wives' salaries is narrowing: After the wife's initially slower career ascendency (due to later schooling and other factors), she is now nearing his rank and the balance of the incomes is shifting. A man in his early 40s, whose wife's salary equals his and is on the rise, grappled with not being the primary breadwinner:

So our salaries now are equal, and next year she'll probably earn more than me. There's a little bit of tense joking about this issue, about who's going to earn more money. It's a highly symbolic thing, I think. It's not going to destroy our marriage if she bests me by $20,000 next year. I am philosophically committed, I think, to the proposition that one's contribution to the world is not measured by salary, and one's success is not measured by salary. And yet, I guess I'm conscious of this, and trying not to be upset by the fact that I've made some choices in choosing this career regarding money not being of prime importance. I guess I find it perplexing that I am noting it. If I'm really honest, I think at some point it would start to bother me. I'm not sure what the breaking point would be, when it would really become an issue.

His wife described:

It's tax time, so we've been joking about money and who made more. I don't think it's serious competition, although I think he'd be a bit put out if I made significantly more money. That hasn't happened yet. In his heart of hearts, something would rankle.

Many men acknowledged that their views on comparative income were bastions of tradition and even chauvinism; discussion of salaries elicited these recognitions more frequently than any other topic in the interviews. A man in his mid-30s explored how he might feel if his wife earned more money:

Ideally I shouldn't feel anything. I probably would feel like I should be earning more—not that I should be getting paid more for what I was doing, but that I should be earning either the same amount or more than her. It's probably the male ego. I guess it's chauvinistic.

In general, when other aspects of a couple's life reflected a traditional reality, so did income. In a couple who maintained a view of his career as more salient than hers, the husband commented: "If she earned more than me, would I feel kept? Would my pride be hurt? I don't know. It's never happened, so I don't know. I think she would worry about the effect it would have on me."

How did men feel when their wives did earn a higher salary? The small number of couples for whom this was true expressed a wide range of responses. For one man, for example, his wife's higher income has been a source of shame and frustration. He reports that over the years he has accommodated somewhat to not living up to the ideal of being a "macho" provider, noting, "If you had asked me these questions six or seven years ago, I probably would have abstained from answering." However, he also proclaimed, "It would make me feel like a million bucks to earn more than she does." His original expectation that the man should earn more than the woman has persisted. In contrast, an academic in his mid-30s seemed not to expect that he should earn more than his wife. He accepted the situation and appreciated his wife's higher income: "It would be nice if I were paid better for what I do. But I'm glad she is paid as well as she is. It keeps me from feeling like I need to support the family single-handed." His wife is equally accepting of the circumstances:

> Bob jokes that I allow him to dabble in research. It's nice to make a good salary, especially as a woman. It gives me a good feeling, a sense of security. I know I could support myself and the children if anything were to happen to Bob.

This knowledge that they could provide if divorce or death removed their spouse's income emerged as a common theme for many women. No man in the sample mentioned this. Another woman with a high salary reported:

> I like those statistics that show that I'm in the top 5% of women in terms of salary, and I hope those ranks grow. It's important to be independent. This is a morbid thought, but if I lost John, I have to know that I could carry on by myself. I saw that when his father died, his mother's financial insecurity drove her right into another marriage. Financial insecurity is a horrible feeling.

Women were often reluctant to admit the importance of money to them. A woman in her upper-30s described:

> It was important to me, in choosing among various career paths that were options to me, to be able to make money. I mean, if something were to happen to Eric, I wanted to know that I could be the breadwinner. I feel myself blushing as I say this—being worried about money, thinking that it is motivation for this career.

There were also women who held a traditional expectation that their husbands should earn more than they, much as they preferred that their husbands be more successful. A woman in her upper-30s stated clearly that she wanted her husband to earn more money than she:

> When he started working, I had been working longer and earned more. There was a lot of checking about money and salary raises. It meant a lot to him when he passed me, and then left me in the dust. It didn't matter to me. It would come up when we got our raises and merit increases. It was fine with me when he started earning more. I liked it that way.

Interestingly, the desire of women for their husbands to earn more than they appeared to be less universal than their wish for their husbands to be more successful than they. Perhaps the impact of unequal salaries is softened by the fact that different fields pay differently. Hence, a higher salary may not mean greater success. The theme of differential salaries across fields emerged frequently in discussions of comparative income. Many participants described frustration, resentment, and anger stemming from inequitable pay across professions that was highlighted by an intimate, on-going exposure to the pay scale of the spouse's profession. A man in his mid-30s reported: "I don't know if I'd be as conscious of how poorly academics are paid if I weren't married to a lawyer. It's hard not to notice that for the same long, hard hours we get paid wildly different amounts."

The relationship of relative pay to power and dynamics within the home is complicated and clearly varies among couples. Does higher income buy certain rights and privileges for a spouse? The answer appears to be: not necessarily. The complaints of the highest paid women about carrying disproportionate responsibility for housework and child care frequently resembled those of women at the lower end of the salary spectrum. However, greater resources can and do buy surrogate help. There appears to be some association between the woman's income and the amount of household and child care help that the family purchases. Notably, this association appears to exist even if the combined resources of the spouses are not greater than couples in which the wife's income is lower. Thus, women who fill the provider shoes more fully may feel more entitled to subcontract their traditional homemaker duties.[12]

The association of relative income to marital and family power was typically subtle. For a few couples, the relationship of salary to roles and power became a highly visible and pivotal leitmotif for the couple. For example, Sam earns substantially more than Ellen and has argued explicitly over the years that this means his wife should carry the homemaker responsibilities. Now in their early 40s, the couple had embarked on the marriage with traditional expectations for division of roles:

> He: Because I was able to make money in my profession, it wasn't that important that she make money. Much of the time, I feel like she's basically doing volunteer work, that I'm supporting her hobby. Since I make so much more than she does, I feel I've held up my end of the

---

[12]Similarly, Lave and Angrist (1975) found, in a sample of working mothers in clerical and managerial positions, that the woman's income was a more important factor than family income in determining how much money was spent on child care.

bargain. So I should be entitled to other rights, namely doing less work around the house. I feel that's her end of the bargain.

She: Because he's able to earn a lot of money at his career, well, there's an equation of money, success, and importance of the career. So when a child was sick, there was no question in his mind of who would stay home because "his job is more important because he makes more money." I fear that what I do is always measured in terms of how much money it earns. I think he means importance in terms of its function to the family, not importance in general. But sometimes it's difficult to sort out. But then again, we wouldn't live the way we do if it weren't for his income. So in some sense, I do feel the old traditional tug of doing my end of the bargain. So I don't push for total equality. I guess it's that I'm looking for what's best within our family.

Money and career importance are not identical. It is possible for a lower paying career to be respected and to hold a position of significance in the family. However, this is far more likely to happen if the lower paying career is the man's. In other words, the traditional perception that the man's career is salient counters the fact that it earns less money. In general, for a woman's career to be viewed as equally salient as her husband's by the couple, it helps for her to earn an income comparable to his.

Spouse's Income and Career Options

As noted earlier, men were more likely than women to perceive their spouse's income as aiding their careers. Most commonly noted was the wife supporting the couple during the husband's graduate education. In addition, several men talked about feeling less pressure regarding the breadwinner role because of their wife's income. Several men spoke of the possibility in the future of making a career move that involved risk and therefore would rely on the wife's income for financial security. However, few men had actually used the wife's income to support such a move. Thus, men described their wife's income as having some psychological impact but had made few actual changes in their career path as a result.

In contrast, many women took career risks that they claimed they would not have taken were it not for the husband's income. It may be that women can benefit from this flexibility provided by the spouse's income because it represents a variant, albeit updated, on the classic male provider role. A woman in her early 30s commented:

I wasn't concerned at all when I decided to change jobs, which involved a 40% decrease in pay. You know, this may be the flip side of what I was saying before, about not having issues regarding earning as much or more than my husband. It has to do with women feeling they can be supported by their husbands. I had the luxury of thinking that, in effect, Mitchell was subsidizing me. And I didn't think twice about whether he should.

Many women expressed a willingness for this increased career flexibility to be symmetrical and for their income to provide a base to enable their husbands to make career moves. A woman in extended postdoctoral training described:

I've been able to work for four years for low pay, because he's provided a secure financial base. In the future, he's talking about trying his own business, and since I'm earning a reasonable amount now, he should be able to.

Her husband also described the possibility of his establishing his own business. In addition, however, he stated that he felt compelled to earn more than his wife, suggesting that he might not permit himself to engage, as she had, in an extended period of low pay work.

Although atypical, one man suggested a way in which his wife's income had hurt his career:

I think her salary has been kind of a detriment at times. It's kind of like welfare. You get in a comfortable niche, so you have less drive, less push. You get complacent. She's said that, too: "If I hadn't gone to work, maybe you'd be further."

Handling Finances

In this sample, two thirds of couples pooled all finances; the other one third handled a substantial amount of their finances separately. Of these, most had some separate and some joint accounts; two couples kept everything separate. The method chosen did not appear to be related to absolute or relative income levels of the husbands and wives nor to ages of the spouses.[13]

In the traditional marriage, property and resources are combined.

---

[13]Keeping finances separate may be associated with two other dimensions of keeping things separate. The decision to keep monies separate did bear some relation to the woman keeping her own last name. (In 40% of the couples, husband and wife had different last names.) Of the couples who kept separate accounts, two thirds had different surnames versus one quarter of the couples who had pooled accounts. In addition, keeping two checking accounts may be related to maintaining two households. The commuting couples in the sample utilized separate finances.

What contributes to a decision to keep finances separate? Personal preferences were strong on both sides of the issue. A woman in a pooled financial marriage declared: "I just think it's really important for two people who are married to share the same pot, whether it's full of fortune or misfortune. I think it'd be weird to have different resources at your disposal." A woman who strongly endorsed their separate finances stated: "We each pay a percentage of the rent, the groceries, the expenses. When I was a teenager, I didn't like having someone else pay for the movies or whatever. I like to pay my own way."

Whether their finances were pooled or separate, couples often designated the two paychecks for different expenses. This delegation seemed to carry some importance in the joint view of the significance of the wife's career. Many men, for example, said the wife's income was useful for certain aspects of family expenses, but that the husband still served as the family's core provider. A man in his early 40s implied that having his wife pay for essential living expenses would be like "living on a dole":

> If she were carrying the financial burden to do the things we really wanted to—like private schools for our kids—then I would feel guilty, bad. I suppose that's chauvinistic. Early in our marriage, I wasn't doing well financially, so it was like that when we lived on a dole from her parents.

A frequent pattern of division of expenses was for the wife's paycheck to be allocated, among other things, for child-care costs. The underlying message, at least for many couples, is that child care is a necessity *because* the woman is employed outside the home. It is as if her income only starts to count above and beyond child-care costs. The repercussions of this view may be significant. One woman who had recently decided to taper back her hours stated: "My income was going for childcare and taxes. So I could decrease work to part-time and we'd still be okay. It didn't end up making that much difference." Similarly, allocation of the woman's paycheck to extras such as vacations and pleasure activities seemed to relegate it to second-class status. The woman's income is viewed as pin money and playful rather than essential for the family's functioning.

In contrast, women who carried responsibility for expenses like mortgage payments and household bills experienced a sense of their vital contribution to the household. A woman in her early 40s noted:

> Even though my income is smaller than Tom's, it's really important that I know my money is going for important things. I like the fact that our family's medical insurance is covered through my job.

Like men, these women occasionally spoke of the burdens and worries accompanying supporting a family but also experienced the satisfaction of providing. A woman in her upper-30s described:

> I never expected to earn this much money. I think it has to do with being a woman. But it feels really good to write the checks each month, and to see that I can help take care of our family.

SUMMARY: TWO CAREERS IN DEVELOPMENT

Let us consider a snapshot of the two careers developing side by side under a single roof. The spouses interact with each other's careers in a number of ways. They talk extensively about their work with each other, sometimes providing guidance about career directions as well as advice about handling day-to-day office politics and substantive questions. Gender differences emerge in both the quantity and quality of work talk. Wives talk about their work more than husbands. Husbands are more prone than wives to give advice about work-related matters, whereas wives are more likely to focus on socioemotional dimensions of work situations. Geographic moves, which comprise a crucial dimension along which spouses can help or hinder each other's careers, continue on average to favor the husband's career. However, a substantial proportion of couples now organize geographic moves around the wife's career as well.

Dual-career spouses provide a live-in point of comparison that appears most likely to generate competitive feelings when one career is not going well. We find that women feel uncomfortable surpassing their husbands in success and that men may feel especially sensitive to issues of comparative income. The enduring expectation is for the man's career to be more important: to earn more money, be more successful, dictate more geographic moves. Importantly, the husband's career also tended to become established before the wife's, due to his earlier choice of a career path and his more immediate move into graduate education. Husband's and wife's ambitions appear somewhat different: He is more likely than she to set highly specific career goals and to have expected to be further along in his career by this point.

Interdependent with the dual developing careers is the shared family life of the two spouses. Many men felt their careers were hindered by their wives' expectations that they help with domestic work, whereas many wives felt that their husbands' lack of involvement at home burdened their careers. Some women also appreciated the ways their careers were facilitated by their husbands' contributions to family work. We now turn to a fuller examination of these interrelationships of the worlds of work and family.

Chapter 4

The Work and Family System

I feel like I have two careers—one at work, and one at home. I see that the energy expended at home clearly rivals that at the office. So I have lots of respect now for women who decide to stay at home. Staying at home for two days feels more stressful than two days at work. [Do you have a sense what the nature of the stress is?] I think it comes from being responsible for two human lives. It's difficult to know if you're doing the right thing. As a parent, there are no answers. At work, there are answers; you can always ask a colleague. Here, you won't know if you're right till 15 years down the line.

—A scientist in her mid-30s

I need long periods of intense thought to ponder an idea, turn it all around, look at it different ways. This is surely a repeat theme in this interview: When you play it back, I must have said a half dozen times how there aren't enough hours in the day. I'm sorry to be so redundant, but it's an important theme. I have a burning desire to do more, to do the best. It's hard to do that, and be home with the kids as much as my wife would like me to be.

—An academic in his early 40s

I'm really looking forward to Jill cutting back a little on work, so that she can be with the kids more. Of course, I suppose I should be considering cutting back too. That's the other side of the coin. And I guess I don't want to, I don't feel I could.

—A lawyer in his mid-30s

In response to a question about what defines health in adulthood, Sigmund Freud is reputed to have offered the now famous response of *lieben und arbeiten*—the ability to love and to work. A description of the dual-career family may look like a full portrait of Freudian health: Both spouses lead lives full of both love and work. In the buzz phrase of our time, these men and women appear to "have it all." But do they really? And if so, how do they do it?

Family life creates demands that compete and often conflict with the demands of work. How do the dual-career spouses balance the spheres of work and family over time, and how do work and family fit together each day? The next two chapters are devoted to examining how work and family influence each other and blend in the life of the dual-career couple.

The dual-career, work-family system is complex on numerous levels. At one level, the pragmatic demands of running a household are enormous. For evidence of this, one need look no further than the nearest full-time housewife; she does not exactly lead a life of leisure. Rather, the tasks of homemaking and child care more than fill a full-time schedule.[13] Without a full-time homemaker, the family faces a major challenge: How can the family, in addition to the two careers, work without a round-the-clock wife and mother?

At another level are questions of investment in family versus work. The full-time homemaker not only did the shopping and swept the floors, but she also put home and family first. No job interfered with or limited the homemaker's focus on children and household. From morning to night, she was available to meet children's needs whenever they were done with school, *their* day's work. The woman's full-time commitment to home and family often balanced and tried to compensate for the man's lack of time for the home, given his commitment of tremendous hours and energy to his career.

Thus, a crude analysis of the home-work system in the dual-career family suggests two types of questions: How do home and work fit together pragmatically, when both spouses are physically absent from the home all day? And how do home and work fit together psychologically, when both spouses have high-commitment careers that reputedly absent them at a psychological level from children and a marriage?

In their research on adult development in men, Levinson and his colleagues (1978) defined the concept of the life structure. Life structure consists of all the ways the individual engages with the world,

---

[13]For example, Oakley (1974) found that housewives with young children worked an average of 77 hours per week in the home.

including work, family, friendships, religion, athletics, community activities, creative pursuits, and so on. Individuals strive, over the course of development, to find a life structure that fits with and allows full expression of the innermost self. Developmental tasks require evaluation of and shifts in the life structure; hence, it is constantly evolving. An important dimension of the life structure is how much attention is devoted to each aspect. Each individual arrives at a relative balance of the components that feels right.

To date, the concept of the life structure has been applied to the psychology of the individual. However, it also provides a useful framework to think about the challenges and issues of the dual-career couple. A marriage involves continual interaction of two individual life structures that may parallel, complement, or conflict with each other. Which issues arise, for example, when spouses view different balances among the various components of the life structure to be ideal?

Each couple has a collective life structure as well as two individual ones. Together, spouses may experience a collective sense of self, and the couple may strive to achieve balance and full expression of the collective self in their joint life structure. In the traditional marriage, the individual life structures of husband and wife appeared quite distinct and complementary. In their *collective* life structure, husband and wife may have experienced a balance of family and work components and of needs for expressivity and agency. In the dual-career marriage, spouses attempt to balance work and family components *within* rather than *across* individual life structures.

THE EFFECT OF FAMILY ON CAREERS

The Competing Pulls of Work and Family

The phenomenology of most dual-career spouses suggests a constant tug-of-war between career and family. Because neither spouse can devote unlimited time to either domain, the question arises of what happens when both spheres require some limits.

Many couples described a heavily work-oriented lifestyle for both spouses before their children arrived. When spouses' work investments were symmetrical, the tremendous amount of time devoted to career and relatively small amount of time for marital and social life was not necessarily deemed problematic. Both spouses of one couple told the story of their aborted attempts to go to the theater together several weeks in a row. One week, the husband showed up for the curtain fall. Another week, he never arrived at all. The husband used the story to illustrate how important it was to have a wife who understood the unpredictable demands of work because of the capricious demands of her own career; the wife good-naturedly exclaimed, "Sometimes it gets a little ridiculous!" The underlying assumption for these couples in their prechildren days was that work demands took precedence and that spouses would understand.

This is not meant to imply that prior to children there are no conflicts about the balance of home and family. When one spouse is more devoted to work than the other, issues certainly arise. Tension is often generated from differential investment of the two spouses in work versus marriage. When there are no children, housework may be a pivotal battleground.

Once there are children, the dual-career family system undergoes a profound shift. The pragmatic demands on the home front increase exponentially and cannot be postponed, rescheduled or ignored. Both men and women depict that it is clearly the children's arrival that creates the greatest conflict between home and career. A woman in her mid-30s described:

> I had worked single-mindedly to establish my career, and put everything else second to that. And then I really did a turn-around when I wanted to have a family. I made that the most important thing. That has changed my career. I would still be working more hours and not minding it—60 or 80 hours a week without a second thought—if I didn't have a child.

For the majority of both men and women, having children translated into fewer hours at work. However, the extent to which this occurred and the meanings of this shift differed for men and women.

It is important to recognize that the issue is *not* simply whether to utilize child care. Full-time child care does not allow most of these professionals to continue their more-than-full-time careers at the pre-child level. Hence, the questions of how to juggle children and careers involve such issues as how to squeeze extra work hours out of a day (e.g., at home in the evening or on the weekends), who will pick up the child from day care and hence have a rigidly fixed end to the work day, and who will care for the child when child care is not an option (when the child is sick or the caretaker is away or ill).

Children and Women's Careers

About two thirds of the women described accommodating their careers to fit their families. For some women, this issue had influenced their choice of career (e.g., insuring a flexible schedule) or of work site. A woman lawyer explained, for example, "I made a very conscious decision to work at this firm because they believed that there was life after law." Other women discovered new pockets of flexibility or "ways to cut corners" (an often-used phrase) on the job. A woman academic in her early 40s described: "When I went into academia, I thought it would give me summers and time off to devote to my research. Now I use that time for my daughter."

A few women in the sample reduced their hours to part time. However, many careers do not provide options for viable part-time work. Many women described their work environments as not willing or able to bend to the demands of family. Several women described hostile reactions from work colleagues to pregnancies. In general, the more a person's career is entrenched in organizational life, the less likely the work setting is to be flexible about intermittent or long-term scheduling accommodations. A businesswoman in her early 40s reported:

> The children will probably be at college before I feel comfortable being out of the house all day Monday to Friday. If I could find a job that was rewarding both vocationally and financially and had a wonderful career path that would go 9 a.m. to 3 p.m.—well, there would probably be a zillion other women ahead of me. I don't think I'll ever resolve what must be inborn guilt to be there and be here too. I just can't be at their school plays. I have to be very choosy about what I can do.

Although the majority of women did not officially reduce their work schedules or workloads, the effects of children on their work schedules were often profound. Some women felt continuously that they wanted more time for work than was available. A woman in medicine, for example, expressed her frustration that she could not attend hospital rounds at 7 in the morning. Most women expressed occasional regrets that they had less time to work than was sometimes necessary or desirable. In addition to influencing the quantity of time at work, accommodating work to children sometimes influenced the shape and direction of women's careers. One woman described that her desire to maintain a flexible schedule precluded career advancement at this time:

> What's important to me at this point is that I control what I do. So being the head of something is out of the question for now, because you can't control it. I guess it's related to my kids, these new priorities. So I don't know about that part of me that wanted to run something. Maybe it'll emerge at some point when I have more time.

Women often depicted their decisions to temper career ambitions as desirable. A woman who had tapered back her work hours reported:

> I used to think I'd cut back to part time for about five years, and then when the kids were in school I'd go back to full time. But now I see that I don't want to do that. I want to be with them because they're *not* toddlers. They're great at this age!

In general, women linked their reduction of work hours to a wish to more actively participate in their children's upbringing. These women experienced frustration at getting so little first-hand exposure to the day-by-day wonders of child development. A woman in her upper-30s described:

> It's like not wanting to fly over cities. I prefer to go by steamboat, see the sights; maybe you have some rough times, but you live it in three dimensions. That's how I like to travel, and that's the kind of mother I want to be.

However, for women who also experienced strong attachments to work, the result is an approach-approach conflict. A physician in her mid-30s stated:

> I am feeling a lot of conflict now about how much time I spend at home with my daughter. My career is important to me, it's very important. But it's not so important that I'm willing to give 60 or 80 or 100 hours per week to it. I want to have a more reasonable amount of time that I work, and then time for my daughter and my husband.

The women in the sample differed widely in terms of the number of hours they considered too many. For some women, cutting back on work meant a reduction from 80 to 60 hours; for others, 40 hours at work felt like too many. One woman, for example, described how her threshold for time away from her children was crossed during a work phase that entailed an extra evening per week plus Saturday mornings:

> When I was away from the kids for those extra hours, I felt like I wanted to be with them. I felt a mixture of yearning with a little guilt, but not much, because I know they're well-entertained and safe without me. But I really like to be with them.

A woman's decision to decrease work hours in order to increase family hours needs to be considered within the broader work-family system. Often, the woman felt that one parent should spend more time with the children and that the husband was not going to volunteer to be the one. A woman in her late 30s described:

> I chose to spend more time with the kids, to nurse them, to see them at lunch hour. It increased after the second child. Once Paul got the job across town, he was around very little, and he wasn't about to do it anyway. I felt they should have at least one parent around.

About half of the women described their decision to taper back on work as integrally linked to the husband's continuation of his work level. Ruth, a woman in her upper-30s, described her decision to cut back on her work:

> We both shared a peak about two years ago. We had both been promoted to positions of high responsibility, and at the same time we realized that we had two kids. So we wondered, do we take off down this very career-oriented path, or does one fall behind? And that was the time when I realized I was the one who was going to fall behind, with respect to careers.

However, even when women described a conscious decision to reduce their work hours and a willing acceptance of the husband's hours remaining the same, conflicts often were triggered by the inequity. Ruth commented:

> Sometimes it's hard not to resent that I take care of everything at home. But I wouldn't want Jason home more if he would end up feeling like he was making sacrifices at work and resenting the time at home. And those points of irritation are less, now that I'm home more. When we were both working full time I felt we should both make efforts to be home more with the kids.

At the heart of these arrangements are the two basic expectations discussed in chapter 2. First, career is viewed as more primary for men than for women. Ruth was asked how she had decided that she was "the one who was going to fall behind":

> His job was much more demanding, he had twice as much to do. Also, even though he consciously didn't admit it, he wouldn't be good to have around the home. He needs to be at work more than I do. So it was a question of assessing our personalities.

Second, family is perceived as more important for women than for men. The majority of women differentiated their balance of work-family from their husbands'. A woman in her mid-30s stated:

> As much as I love my work, and I really do, the family comes first with me. And that's different for George—work is more important for him. Like in spare moments at home, he works. I don't. I feel that's time with the kids.

A woman in her early 40s commented:

> It's hard for me when I can't get to the kids' school functions. I think it's different for John. I think he sees it through a more traditional male perspective, so he would not see lack of time with the kids as a disadvantage of dual careers.

About one quarter of the women described some reluctance to share parenting equally and expressed a desire to retain dominance over the domain of children. A woman in her upper-30s reported:

> I was very ambivalent before deciding to have a child regarding slowing down my career. But I can't give up controlling her, and fully share it with Jay. She's my responsibility. It's true for all the parents I see. No matter how well-educated we all are, this isn't changing that rapidly. Like I know a woman physician who leaves clothes out for her husband to dress their daughter.

Children and Men's Careers

Men fully corroborated their wives' views that children influence the women's careers more than their own. This recognition was presented in a matter-of-fact way. The men tended to be sympathetic observers but not to cast themselves as active participants in their wives' accommodation of careers for their children. A man in his mid-30s reported:

> Kids pose a far more severe problem for women in terms of career advancement, no matter how well-intentioned the man is. In cases like mine, the man is going to go in to work with circles under his eyes and be a little less productive, but no one is going to really notice. With the woman, she'll take more time off work and if the child is sick, she'll stay home. We're fairly even about child care, but not 50/50.

A man in his upper-30s commented:

> The balance is much harder for her. She is trying to develop a career at the same time as participating in social change. For a woman with young children, the ideal would be to work 70% time, but there's no precedent for that. So she needs to be 100% in both places, which is unrealistic. [How about for you? Are there problems from being involved in social change?] No, not really.

Interestingly, the husbands were more focused than their wives on how children can interfere with women's careers. Perhaps this again reflects the male assumption that careers are primary, so that children are more likely to be seen by men than women as a challenge to swift career development. Women may have a greater investment than men in children that balances any hindering effects that children may have on career development. Alternatively, women may feel more reluctant, perhaps due to expectations of the importance of family to them, to experience or express the view that children have hampered their career growth. Still another interpretation is that women attribute the difficulties not to having children but rather to their husbands' limited involvement in childrearing.

The majority of men differentiated their feelings of conflict over family and career from their wives' feelings. The husbands reasoned that these differences stemmed from the expectations of work as primary for men and family as primary for women. For example, a man in his mid-30s stated:

> I have the suspicion that it's more difficult for a woman. If you're a traditional, career-oriented man, you're supposed to spend a lot of time in the office, and bring work home, and commute long distances. And the man has less time for the family, which is not a good thing, but that's how it is traditionally. Whereas for a woman, there's always the other side of the mirror, which is the woman who is at home, spending hours and hours with her children, and is always there when they need her. And that imposes some degree of guilt on a woman who is successful in her career.

Men also linked the differential conflicts to persisting differences in the family responsibilities of men and women. A man in his upper-30s described:

> Sure, occasionally I feel I ought to spend more time with our kids. Or because I'm preoccupied by my work, I don't listen as well as I ought to. But I feel a lot less of that than Joyce does. It's not that it's an overriding concern for her, but it's there. From what I've read and what she's read, it's something that a lot of career women have to deal with. Women still have the other things to do; they don't disappear because they're working.

Men rarely conveyed the sense that they wanted their wives to work more hours, if the wife were part time or full time but "cutting corners." Rather, they corroborated their wives' views that the men would be unlikely candidates for working reduced hours. Similar to the women's explanations of this asymmetry, the salience of work to the male identity formed the core of the men's arguments on this issue. A man in his early 30s described: "If one of us were going to cut back on work, it would be very unlikely to be me. I wouldn't want to do it because, for me, my career is as important as my family." A man in his early 40s, whose wife had recently decided to scale back on work, elaborated on this view that his career is an essential and primary element of his life structure:

> A career is a necessity. You need to earn money, and you have to be successful. Otherwise, you'll end up moving all the time, and losing self-respect. A marriage is a luxury. It's something that will make you happy, like having a good meal with good wine with friends. You need the money from the career to buy the meal, and even though I know this is simplistic, you probably need the career to enjoy the marriage.

A consistent picture thus evolves of women more than men accommodating their careers to family. However, the arrival of children had an impact on husbands' work lives as well. Many men described working a significantly greater proportion of their hours at home, during the evening, the very early morning, and the weekend. A man in his early 30s described how he has reduced his work hours since the birth of his child. Typical of many, he reports now working 45 hours in the office rather than the 60-70 he did before the child, and then working another 10-15 hours at home:

> It's been interesting. I want to do it, have to, there's no choice. It's been challenging. I need to figure out a way to get just as much done, and keep just as thorough control over things. I'm sure it's a set of techniques you learn, of delegating different kinds of work to other people, and being able to think about things in the shower. I'm getting there, slowly.

Some men described a considerable challenge in giving up the flexibility of their previous work schedules. A man in his mid-30s described:

> I'm a very high energy person, and I like to get to work early. But when you have a family, you have to adjust. There are other people involved. Even if you're the nominal head of the household, you have no power over that.

Several men also described the ways having a family balanced some of their work-oriented tendencies. A man in his early 40s noted:

Dual-career marriages without children are very different. They may be less stable, because children keep us involved with the home. Otherwise, we'd be more involved with work, outside activities, etc.

In addition, men depicted a number of situations in which they had adapted their work situation to child care. Interestingly, they said these adaptations had positive as well as negative effects on their work life. It might be predicted that men receive more hostile reactions than women for child-care interferences with work, because child care represents out-of-role behavior for men. However, its nontraditional nature may prove advantageous. In the current social climate, involved fathers may reap benefits from—or at least be tolerated for—their involvement with their children. Whereas a woman whose child inter-feres with her work life is confirming all the worst fears about employed women, a man in the same situation may be seen as progressive. A few men related instances of this. Furthermore, because many of the men's careers are more strongly established than their wives', they may be able to take more liberties. A man in his upper-30s described a recent scenario:

The baby was sick, and Joan was presenting at a meeting. So I brought the baby to a meeting with me. I guess she was not exactly warmly received, but I can get away with it because I'm at this stage in my career. Joan can't do that at her point in her career.

THE SPHERES OF WORK AND FAMILY

Asymmetry in the Balance of Work and Family

For one third of the couples, differences in the degree that wives and husbands accommodated their careers for children became a central marital tension. For these couples, differential investment in career and family is the recurrent issue around which arguments occur, and it demands constant renegotiation. In the framework of the life structure, these are spouses who define a different balance of components to be optimal: She would like them separately and collectively to devote a bigger slice of the pie to family than he would.

In the traditional, one-career marriage, the husband's involvement in career represents a huge discrepancy with the wife's lack of career. One might predict that the dual-career arrangement, with both spouses pursuing high-commitment careers, would reduce such tensions. As described earlier, about half of the husbands explicitly desired a dual-career marriage. Many men assumed a wife with her own career would lessen her time demands on them. This expectation was realized for some couples: A work-involved spouse permitted the other spouse to indulge in his or her work without creating an imbalance.

However, a reverse effect is also possible. The assumption of the one-career family is that the man's role is to involve himself in career to provide for the family. Hence, a full-time homemaker's complaints that her husband is unavailable to the family may be muffled by the societal view that the work-preoccupied man is upholding "his end of the bargain." There is little expectation that the man carry responsibility for housework or child care, and he is free to work. In the dual-career marriage, both spouses arrive at their own definition of what is required for work success and what level of involvement in the family feels right. In the dual-career marriage, then, each person argues from personal experience about the appropriate balance of work and family, whereas in the one-career marriage, the spheres of wife and husband are less comparable.

For the one third of the couples troubled by this issue, a double standard emerged. Women felt that their husbands should do as they did: cut back on work and devote more time to family. Husbands were in favor of the wives' increased devotion to family but did not feel that a parallel move was feasible or desirable for them.

The repercussions of this imbalance are multiple. First, women who felt that their husbands worked too much expressed concern about the limited time that the husbands spent with the children. The absent father phenomenon, a classic aspect of the male breadwinner-female homemaker family, is no longer deemed acceptable by many. A woman in her mid-30s described:

> If the littlest one wakes in the middle of the night, and Al comes in, that won't do. It's "I want Mommy." That's really a problem, and Al doesn't like it. But the reality is I'm there for him so much more than Al is.

In addition to concerns that the children do not receive adequate attention from their fathers, the wives often feel neglected themselves. Paula, a woman in her mid-30s, explained:

> I find myself wondering whether he's married to his work or to me. I used to feel a fair amount of jealousy around whether he was going to choose to work or to be with me. And when we were together, he would be distracted. He glazes over, and I know he's started to think about work. So then there's a tension of how present the person is, even if he's physically present.

Although Paula is actively engaged in her career, their differing levels of involvement and their differential ranking of career and family are marked. Like other charged issues, such as competition and comparison, the tensions surrounding an asymmetrical investment in work find natural expression in the division of household and child care tasks. Paula continued:

> This issue—of does he care more about his work than his family—always gets translated into all the daily schedules and how the household is run—errands, taking kids to the doctor, etc.

The dynamic produced by differential balance of work and family is a difficult one for couples. One couple described having entered marital therapy because of this issue. Many women feared that a fine line existed between being assertive about their own needs and their children's needs and being perceived in classic female roles as "a nag" or "a shrew." In their struggles for equality and symmetry within the family, women often feared that they were occupying a classic female role that involved complaining, demanding more attention, and feeling frustrated at a situation that often felt out of their control. One woman described her feelings about constantly striving to set limits on her husband's work time:

> It produces tension for me. At the worst times, the tension is, am I dragging him down so that he can't meet his need for success? And we get so mad at each other. Like he wants to take a shorter vacation, so that he's away from work less. I think that's terrible. I think a family vacation should come first.

The themes in these running arguments have a traditional basis: The woman asserts the importance of family life, whereas the man emphasizes the primacy of work. However, women felt that they were petitioning for something nontraditional: the increased valuing of and involvement in family life by men.

Men often felt misunderstood or underappreciated by their wives' demands that they participate more actively in the home and family. Men argued that their wives were unsympathetic to the necessity of their long work hours. All of the men in this subgroup of couples expressed a yearning for more time to do their work to the standards that they desired. An academic described the tension generated by reducing his work hours to accommodate his wife:

> I feel like if you combine intelligence with long hours, that's how the really significant accomplishments are achieved. That is cut off from me,

because my spouse does not agree that I should work those long hours. I compensate by being well-organized, efficient, intuitive. I suppose what I would wish for is to have three hours more per day to work, to achieve my potential—but also to have a happy family. Maybe that's not realistic.

Implicit in his comments is a common male version of having it all— that is, to work as many hours as he would like but also to have a satisfying family life.

Over half of this group of husbands felt that they *did* contribute a significant amount to the family, even if not as much as their wives. They felt they made substantial efforts to accommodate the family and resented the underappreciation and criticism they still received from their wives. One man described his solution after many years of this recurrent theme:

Basically, I do what I have to do to keep Karen happy, so that she's not mad at me, so that I can work. Recently, the rules are explicit and I stick to them, so I'm not in the doghouse. We still haggle over the details.

Although fewer in number than couples where the wife felt that the husband worked too much, there were a few couples in which the husband felt that the wife worked too much. This emerged in couples even where the husband still worked more hours than the wife. The standing joke, with a jointly admitted underlying truth, between a male academic who worked about 80 hours a week and his wife, an internist who worked about 50 hours a week, was that he wished she could have gone into dermatology with its more predictable and more limited hours. Another man described a period where he contemplated marital separation: "When I was thinking of it, it was because of a feeling that her career had become the most important thing in her life. And I felt like I was making sacrifices that she wasn't."

It is crucial to recognize that asymmetry between husbands and wives in their respective balances of work and family does not necessarily produce tension. The key is whether at least one spouse holds an expectation that is distinct from the reality. For some couples, the wife's greater devotion of time and energy to home and child care is mutually acceptable. For some couples, it serves to maintain or reinstate the comfort of the status quo, and needs to be considered within the context of the reluctance of women as well as men to have wives' careers surpass their husbands'. For example, one man's work hours had dramatically increased following a recent job change; prior to this job change, he had envied his wife's relatively greater career acceleration. His wife was willing to absorb almost all of the domestic responsibilities so he could experience a renewed sense of occupational success. She was asked about her reactions to his now much-extended work hours:

> It's not a problem. He was home more before, but less happy, so that cast a shadow over everything. I think it would be very different with little kids; it would be very hard to not be able to share all those tasks. But it's okay for me right now.

Her allusion to the ages of their children underscores an important point. The pragmatic burdens of child care and women's demands for their husband's help are clearly greatest when the children are young. Hence, tensions around asymmetrical balance of work and family may be stronger during certain phases of the family life cycle than others.

The Interface of Home and Work

The temporal boundary between work and family is a complex one, and people manage it in very different ways. Even the assignment of the line varies: Does it occur when the person walks out of the house, during the car ride, upon arrival at the workplace? A woman described:

> When the kids were young, I would think about them on the car ride into work and then coming home. I would drive very fast. When at work, I would leave that behind and get absorbed into the day.

A common metaphor that people used was *switching on and off*:

> When I get to the office, I switch off thinking about family and switch on thinking about work.

> He seems to be able to leave work behind, to switch it off much better than I do.

> I come home and often find it difficult to make that switch from worker into wife.

Another way that people discussed the boundary was in terms of *changing gears*:

> One of the wonderful things about the family and coming home is that you have to shift gears and leave work behind, or at least most of it most of the time. And if things are nuts at home, I'm more than happy to go into the office. You have no choice but to shift gears.

The quantity of time that spouses spend discussing their careers with each other already suggests that the dual-career spouses do not leave work at the office. Our focus now turns to other kinds of crossover of the work-family membrane. How does one domain spill over psychologically into the other? (These analyses of the influx of home into work and work into home do *not* include concrete carry-over, such as bringing a briefcase of work home or making a phone call during the workday about a domestic matter.)

Influx of Work Into Home. For the great majority of dual-career spouses, work does not stay at the office. Almost all the women and the men reported that they bring work home with them. In addition to the discussions about work that spouses have with each other, spillover from work to home includes many less self-controlled influences.

A common way that work follows people home is that the tenor of the work day affects mood at home. To the extent that time at work engenders feelings of frustration, anger, or depression (or of elation, pride, or pleasure), most people say these emotions are *not* simply switched off when they enter the house. These work-related emotions have the potential to color the evening at home and may be displaced onto family members, as John, a man in his early 40s, described:

> You bring home into protected environments, into protected relationships, those feelings you wouldn't display with other people. So when you're annoyed about something that's taken place at the office, you come home in a bad mood and then find ways to divert that bad mood into something that's irrelevant. So a small thing at home turns into a big fight, so it releases tension that has to do with what's going on at work.

A troubling work situation therefore can produce ripple effects at home. These ripples may be viewed as *catharsis*: As John described, the argument over a trivial domestic matter may provide an outlet for tension that has been brewing all day. Alternatively, the carry-over of office tensions into the home environment may be seen as *contamination*: Rather than providing a change of atmosphere, the home environment replicates office tensions.

In addition to problems that may arise from the carry-over of emotions and moods, difficulties arise when work environment styles of interaction are imported into the family. Different kinds of work foster development of different perspectives for viewing the world and different methods for doing things. The overflow of these work-related approaches into the home was commented on by about one third of the women and a couple of men. Intrusion of work style into the home may be triggered by a particular day's events, as a woman lawyer described:

> Being in court is very combatative. If I've been dumped on all day, or feeling frustrated with an uncooperative witness, I come home in a combatative mood. It makes me a less than pleasant person to be with.

Typically, work styles become deeply ingrained, and they may render a repetitive or chronic influence. A woman scientist described how skills that were essential for and adaptive in her work setting clashed in the family environment:

> When I'm at work, I am, and need to be, incredibly detail-oriented and organized. If something is out-of-place, it might totally botch up an experiment. Then I come home, and nothing is in place! If I think that I can control things and people at home, I get into real trouble. So I need to not let it bother me. I need to remind myself that work and home are totally different.

As reported in the last chapter, spouses tended to talk more about the wife's work than the husband's. Perhaps related to this, men said they needed more time for private reflection about work while at home than did women. Thoughts about work included both content (ideas for a paper or solutions for a project) and process (office politics or personnel issues). Time away from the immediate stresses of the work environment was seen as a valuable opportunity to sort things through. A man in his early 40s described:

> I definitely bring work home. I don't always discuss it, but I require time privately to work it out. The pressure is so huge—feelings, money, travel, etc. It's tough for Jane to deal with it, so I spare her and keep it to myself.

A man in his upper-30s commented on how he "steals time" at home for reflection on work:

> The problem when I'm at home is that occasionally my kids will find me in a flight of fancy. Invariably it's that I'm thinking about my work. And the kids will say, "Wake up, Daddy."

Influx of Home Into Work.   The majority of both men and women, then, find that their work lives enter into and render an influence over their home lives. Men and women differ in the extent to which the opposite is true. Although women as well as men felt that the influence of work on home was stronger than the effect of family on work, carry-over from home to work was reported by about half the women but only a few men.

Family life is transported into the work sphere in several ways that parallel the carry over of work into the home. First, family issues are discussed with co-workers, much as work issues are processed with spouses. Women's greater propensity to discuss their families with co-workers seems to complement women's greater inclination to discuss their work at home. A woman physician described: "I talk a lot with other women doctors and nurses about all of these issues about home and family. I get a lot of support from that."

Much as the mood of a work day can permeate the home boundary, so too can troubles or joys from home influence feelings at work. A primary effect is some distraction and reduced ability to concentrate. A businesswoman commented: "I notice that when things haven't gone well at home, I don't concentrate as well. My productivity goes down." Most of the time, this influence was described as a minor, temporary intrusion. In general, people reported that their domestic lives were less consistently stressful than their work lives. Some participants clarified that events at home tended to be mildly stressful ("like background noise," described one man) but did not demand contemplation or processing during work hours. In addition, both male and female participants depicted the structured nature of the work environment and their high level of immersion in the day's work as reducing home's influence on work. On occasions where more serious problems have arisen in the family sphere, the effects tend to be more noticeable and significant. A man reported: "When she miscarried, we both felt very upset. I screwed up on a job around then, and I'm sure that's why. I just wasn't all there."

Separation of Home and Work. Interestingly, some men and women described separation of home and family as ideal. About one third of the women made conscious efforts not to bring home into work. Few of these women actually experienced carry-over from home to work. The women who strove to leave family issues at home feared that carry-over of home to work would be seen as unprofessional and would be held against them. In their typically male-dominated work worlds, these women strove to attain the male model of competence that they perceived as involving a one-way (home to work) barrier. A woman in business described a recent instance:

> Last Wednesday, the baby got a very bad flu for the first time. My babysitter called me at work. The next day I had a major presentation— a three-hour talk to be videotaped for national distribution. I delegated some tasks, and told my boss I'm going to have to go home. I said, I'll put the slides together at home tonight, and we won't have time to go over them as we had planned, but I'll see you tomorrow. And then I wrote the

talk till 2 a.m., and the baby got up at 4. I don't want to brag, but no one knew. The meeting was with these guys in the organization that were very high up, so I wasn't going to say, "Oh, guess what I did last night with my baby." It was really important to keep them separate.

Men echoed the ideal that home should not infiltrate work but were less likely to discuss it as an explicit or conscious goal. It is possible that men simply assume that home should not come into work. One man noted this explicitly: "I think the company communicates that if you're too involved in personal interests or family, you're probably not working hard enough." In contrast to the women, who often feel that they need to *prove* that home and family do not interfere with their work, men do not feel an implicit accusation to overcome.

Unlike their wives, a subgroup of husbands take the ideal a step further in wishing to compartmentalize home and work in both directions. Although few men and women reported a lack of carry-over from work to home, one third of the men articulated that they would *like* to keep the two spheres separate. One man responded that he "dislike(s) there to be contagion between the two." A male lawyer described:

I try to keep them very separate, which is my preference. I don't bring work home unless I'm really annoyed about something. It's better to leave work at the office.

MAKING THE SYSTEM WORK

Time

Nearly every dual-career spouse proclaims that time is one if not *the* primary problem that they face. Answers about time are almost universal in response to questions like, "What are the disadvantages of the dual-career marriage?" or "What aspects of your dual-career marriage would you most like to change?" Many feel a shortage of time at both work and home. A man in his early 40s described how he tried to improve time management in both spheres:

The thing I keep coming back to is the need for time. Not that you can generate more time per se, but at least you can use it in more gratifying ways. So at home, we just got an *au pair* girl, so we need to do less of the repetitive, petty chores around the house. And at work, I sat down with my secretary to try to increase her doing the things she should do so that I don't need to. I needed to slow down, take a look at my life. It gets to the point where things are so frantic, you don't even know what you're doing.

The spouses focused primarily on two dimensions of their complex day-to-day schedules. They repeatedly strove to convey the hectic pace of their lives. A woman in her mid-30s reported:

> I think you'd need a video camera to really capture what the house is like. It's incredibly hectic. Everyone's rushing around in the morning, getting dressed, getting the kids dressed, [eating] breakfast, [deciding] who is going to take the kids to school and day care, and so on.

They also noted that their lives feel highly scheduled, and that these schedules, although necessary, feel constraining. The time limits of work and family are interdependent rather than separate. The time constraints of one domain produce tension in the other domain that increases the pressure of the first, and so on. A man in his upper-30s commented:

> Deadlines are hard for me, and they're always right there—like picking up the kids at day care at 5 every day. You need to cut conversations short, or whatever is necessary, to get there. It wouldn't be so bad on a short-term basis, but day in, day out over the years, it starts nibbling away at your existence.

A woman in her early 40s remarked:

> Everything is structured. You're constantly structuring: the house, like making sure the cupboards are stocked and the kids are set; and the job, taking care of the office, etc. The real problem is fatigue—I think that will always be the enemy of working mothers.

Hence, the day-to-day and week-to-week pressures of time are salient and impressive in the world of the dual-career marriage. At a broader level, these couples are engaged in a tightly scheduled developmental era of their lives. In the traditional marriage, the early adult years comprise a particularly full era, entailing establishment of both the husband's career and a family. In the dual-career marriage, one more major task is added: establishing not one but two careers. Rather than splitting the tasks of career and family, as was largely true in the one-career marriage, each dual-career spouse tries to do both. Each strives to move up from the low and middle rungs of the career ladders during these crucial early years that typically set the pace for later ascendancy. At the same time, they are conscious of the ticking away of the biological clock. Although delayed childbearing represents one attempt to stagger these tasks, professionals who have engaged in extended graduate education often find that early career stages and early family development still coincide.

In the complex system of two careers, a marriage, and a family, how is time allocated? Where are corners cut? What are the tensions that emerge from the time constraints of the dual-career couple?

Personal Time.   Time for the self was often described as sacrificed in the dual-career family system. A woman in her upper-30s commented: "Neither of us has time for leisure activities. I can't say when I last did a leisure activity. We're both totally goal-directed." Women reported the lack of personal time more than men did. This tendency can be conceptualized in life structure terms. Women are, in effect, wishing for a different balance of components in their life structure than at present with more time for themselves. Perhaps this gender difference relates to intergenerational change and expectations. For men, the long-standing tradition is for a schedule full of work and family commitments. Although for many men increased involvement in the home limits their hours in the office, they do not complain of a shortage of personal time. For women, the highly scheduled career-family combination represents a marked increase in *scheduled* hours (although not necessarily in *busy* hours) over the lives of the previous generation of women. It also may be that women actually have less time to themselves than their husbands because they carry greater domestic responsibilities.

Life in the dual-career family permits little slack for personal indulgence or time off. This contributes to a frequently described fantasy of time to do nothing or time for a favorite but neglected activity. One woman exclaimed, "I would love to have an afternoon to be bored!" A woman in her mid-30s responded to the question, "What aspects of your dual-career marriage would you most like to change or improve?" this way:

> What I would like is to have a few more hours in the day. [What would you do with a few more hours?] I'd love to relax after work before I start cooking dinner, or go to the gym and swim. When I went to pick the kids up yesterday, I had a cake in the oven. Heaven forbid that I get stuck in traffic! I'd love to not have to be somewhere at a certain time. The kids get whatever time we have, so they're not compromised. It's each of us that gets compromised.

The line between leisure as a luxury and taking care of one's own needs as a necessity seems unclear at times. In the traditional family, the woman often put the family first by sacrificing her own needs.

Might the dual-career woman be perpetuating this scenario, albeit with a new wrinkle, as she gives her own needs lower priority than her family's? This may at some level seem implausible or ironic, given the high commitment to career and apparent self-actualization of these women. However, some examples suggest that under the real pressures of time in the dual-career family, some women are making choices that they regret and feel unhappy about. A woman in her mid-30s described how she no longer attends church:

> I like to go to church whereas Peter doesn't, so I've always gone by myself. In this last period of time, during which I've been working so much, I've been reluctant to give up three hours on Sunday of the very little precious time we would have together as a family. So it's another way I've sacrificed my own time to have time together.

Social Life. Half the spouses lamented a lack of time for maintaining established friendships and initiating new relationships. A man in his early 40s described:

> If we've had to cut somewhere in terms of things that one can do in life, the real cut is in socializing. In the past year, maybe twice we've had people over for dinner, and we used to do that quite a bit. So that feels like a real cost of the dual-career situation.

Many men and women also described a lack of time for individual (as distinguished from marital) friendships. A man in his upper-30s commented:

> I have time for work, my kids, my wife—but not time for bowling buddies, drinking buddies, softball buddies. I could use one or two really good friends. Maybe when I get a little older, that will fill back in. I can't imagine going to my grave with as little in the way of friendships as I have right now. I think that would be kind of sad.

All the dual-career couples socialize primarily, and some couples exclusively, with other dual-career couples. The exceptions tend to be couples met through children, as one woman in her early 30s remarked:

> Before we had children, all our friends were dual-career. Since we had kids, we've become friends with some parents through the kids, couples where the woman doesn't work outside the home. Now that I have kids, I have something in common with them. Before, I didn't have anything to relate to.

Approximately half of the socializing done by the dual-career couples occurs with friends from the spouses' work and about half from nonwork environments. Of the work-derived friendships, more were met through the women's work than men's. Where the couples' friends came more from her work environment than his, spouses tended to make a gender-based attribution. One man commented, "Men have fewer social skills in supporting each other in careers than women do." A woman explained, "It's because I, like most women, get much closer to my friends." Interestingly, when the man's work setting provided more friendships than the woman's, the attributions tended to be environmental. A woman described, "His office has more social functions, so you get to know people better."

Participants were asked whether other dual-career couples influenced how the couple thinks about or works out their dual-career marriage. Approximately two thirds of spouses said they had no dual-career role models. Spouses described using their dual-career friends and colleagues as a source of support and ideas but distinguished them from role models. Typical was one man's comment that "There's one couple we've watched struggle with the dual-career situation over the years, but it's more like we commiserate than that it's instructional." A woman commented:

> Practically all our friends are dual-career families, so the jokes we share and the black humor we share is all based on running life in the fast lane. There's the laughing through your tears kind of thing—like you can't believe someone's going to come into your house which seems so dirty that the housing authority could close it down, but it doesn't faze anyone, because that's what their house looks like too.

Many spouses who felt that they had no dual-career role models explained the ways in which they felt different from other dual-career couples in terms of the division of domestic labor, the relative salience of the two careers, the time spent with children, and so on. In addition, many spouses spoke of negative role models, particularly with respect to childrearing issues. A woman remarked, "We watch all these dual-career couples, and see how messed up their children seem, and ask ourselves what we need to do differently."

The third of the spouses who felt they had dual-career role models described both specific and general purposes that they had served. A woman described:

> There are lots of dual-career couples we know with kids about the ages of ours. Someone will solve a particular problem, and word gets around. So

there's a lot of support within the group. Like two other couples got *au pair* girls, and we're thinking of trying that now.

Couples also described problems with having role models, resulting from comparing themselves to an ideal. A woman described:

I think I always look for the ways other couples work things out, which is both good and bad. I'll see a man who seems like an ideal husband, sharing responsibility for things. I try to take it in and sift through it, not wish we could be just like that. Then it's more helpful.

Managing the Domestic Sphere

It is often said that men have long led lives full of both career and family, so why can't women? However, it is crucial to recognize that full of career and full of family are not symmetrical parts of the traditional male equation. It is only now, as their working wives press men to contribute more fully to family life, that the question is being raised: Can women *or* men lead lives full of both work and family? If so, what changes are necessary? Who will do the work at home to which women of the previous generation devoted full-time energy?

The Division of Domestic Labor. In the traditional marriage, men attended to the outer world where money was generated whereas women focused on the interior world of the home. Within the domestic sphere, certain tasks were targeted as suitable to men—such as yard-work, home repairs, and car maintenance (again focusing largely on the outer world)—whereas women attended to the core of domestic life—clothing, cleaning, cooking, and child care. Societal and parental models reinforced this nearly universal picture of the traditional division of roles.

Many of the dual-career couples recognize that, despite the wife's foray into the world of work, they replicate in their own marriage much of the traditional division of labor. Sam, a man in his upper-30s, described:

When it comes down to it, I'm not the one who loses sleep over whether one child needs new shoes or the other needs to go to the dentist. That, to some extent, is sexist. It's a matter of growing up with certain role models. My mom took care of those things. I guess, deep down, I expect Dawn to take care of them. And Dawn, deep down, really expects me to take care of the car, worry about whether it needs servicing, make the appointment. Or when mechanical things break around the house, even though in principle she could get out the screwdriver, in practice I'm the one who does it. So we do carry on some sex roles, even though we share a lot.

Both husbands and wives felt that men were contributing significantly more to the domestic sphere than their fathers had and than many of them had expected. Nonetheless, on average, the bulk of the domestic work still appeared to be conducted by women.

This impression was corroborated by couples' responses to a written questionnaire about who does specific domestic tasks: the husband, wife, or another (such as a housekeeper). (The results are presented in Table 4.1.) The contributions of husbands and wives were approximately equivalent on two school-related tasks (monitoring homework and going to school conferences) and two household chores (vacuuming, which was largely performed by hired help, and washing dishes). Husbands carried responsibility for executing three traditionally male tasks: home repairs, lawn and garden maintenance, and arranging car repairs. Although spouses roughly shared responsibility for preparing breakfast and lunch, wives performed the major portion of other meal-related tasks: planning meals, grocery shopping, and cooking dinner. Wives performed the bulk of child-care tasks: getting children up and dressed, taking care of children alone, taking children to appointments, staying home with a sick child, getting children ready for bed, and making purchases for children. In addition, wives orchestrated the meta-level managerial tasks: arranging for child care, giving directions to housekeeper and babysitter, and making appointments for children.

The overall picture is that a gender-linked division of roles within the home endures. However, these averages do not reflect change over time nor individual differences.

The Evolution of Roles. Despite the lack of universal change, a more co-equal division of labor has evolved over time for many couples. In one third of the couples, the spouses shared (at least a 40/60 split) two thirds or more of the chores traditionally carried by the female. What precipitated these changes, and how do couples divide chores when gender-role traditions are not followed?

Some couples felt that the arrival of children had propelled them into more egalitarian role sharing. When asked how the division of roles had evolved in her marriage, an administrator in her early 30s described:

Evolved is really the right word, from me doing everything to that being halved. We were married for over five years before our daughter was born, and before that I don't think he knew whether he had a clean shirt. He could depend that I had cleaned the shirts and his suits. He'd occasionally go to the grocery store, but the traditional things were something he did not have to worry about. He had his shoes heeled before he knew they were down.

With the coming of our daughter, there were more things to get done, and he started taking over more. And with my increasing job demands, he has come halfway to the middle.

TABLE 4.1
Division of Chores

	% Performed by Wife	% Performed by Husband	% Performed by Other*
Meals			
1. Prepares breakfast	44/46 **	56/47	2/7
2. Prepares lunch	41/47	31/23	27/31
3. Prepares dinner	61/54	30/31	9/15
4. Plans meals	71/64	26/31	3/5
5. Does grocery shopping	61/63	33/31	6/6
Daily child-care tasks			
6. Awakens/dresses child	59/55	29/27	12/18
7. Takes care of child alone	56/49	31/32	13/12
8. Gets child ready for bed	57/55	35/35	9/9
Special child-care tasks			
9. Stays with sick child	49/59	24/22	27/19
10. Takes child to appointments	75/71	22/20	3/9
11. Makes purchases for child	76/79	22/18	2/2
School-related child care			
12. Monitors child's homework	51/40	46/45	3/14
13. Goes to school conferences	54/52	46/48	0/0
Other domestic tasks			
14. Washes dishes	45/42	45/35	12/18
15. Does vacuuming	14/14	15/16	71/70
16. Does other cleaning	16/19	8/9	75/73
17. Does sewing/mending	65/64	19/18	12/13
18. Pays bills	67/67	33/33	0/0
Organizational tasks			
19. Arranges child care	81/73	19/21	0/0
20. Directs babysitter/housekeeper	78/82	22/17	0/1
21. Makes appointments for child	81/81	18/16	1/4
Home repair, car, yard			
22. Arranges car repairs	33/40	67/59	0/1
23. Does home repairs	11/19	79/63	10/19
24. Lawn and garden work	23/24	59/55	18/21

*"Other" primarily refers to housekeepers, babysitters, and other hired help.

**The first number in each column represents the average of the wives' estimates, and the second number in each column represents the average of the husbands' estimates. The agreement between husbands' and wives' estimates averaged 83%.

In contrast, children precipitated a more gender-typed division of chores for other couples. A woman in her mid-30s described:

> Once the kids came, our roles became much more stereotyped. Since I get home from work earlier, I'm expected to cook. Before the kids, we would get home at about the same time, and cook together.

In general, increased domestic work load (e.g., more children) does not appear sufficient to promote change in the gender-role division of labor. Fathers may involve themselves in child care without renegotiating who handles the other chores. Occasionally, turning points in the family life cycle (e.g., the arrival of a child) converge with more ideological changes that affect expectations. A man in his early 40s remarked:

> When our first child was born, things really changed. Before that, if I cooked a meal on a weekend, it was something special, a big deal. When Chris was born, I began to share a lot of the jobs at home—cooking, cleaning, and all. It was right at the time of feminism, and we were surrounded by a community of people that were involved in these issues.

Couples ranged widely in the degree to which they found their division of labor satisfactory. If expectations and reality match, little dissonance is created even if the division appears lopsided to the outside observer. Lynn, a woman in her early 40s who expressed traditional views about her husband's career remaining more primary than her's, reported:

> I do most of the household stuff, and have for most of our marriage. I'm fine with that. And I don't like it when he does the shopping with the kids. They don't do it right, so I can't really grumble if I choose to do it myself.

However, when expectations move away from dividing roles according to gender traditions, a change process is initiated. Regardless of whether expectations change prior to or during a marriage, it is invariably within the context of the marriage that a new model of household management is reached. Even when an egalitarian ethic is endorsed in principle by spouses at the outset of the marriage, the evolution of an egalitarian division of labor takes time, effort, and practice.

With few exceptions, the source of initiation is the wife, as her expectations about the role of work in her life change and she develops a different vision of roles within the domestic sphere. Merely introducing the issue of role sharing does not produce results. The process of renegotiating deeply entrenched patterns is an iterative cycle, laden with affect. The wife is typically not only the initiator of change but also the enforcer. Roger, a man in his upper-30s, reported: "My wife does play the role of enforcer of the family contract, you might say. And I'm grateful to her, because I like being this involved in my son's upbringing." Gratitude may be an ultimate response but is rarely the immediate reaction. Several women spoke of needing to refuel the courage of their convictions in the face of their husbands' resistance and anger and their own frustration and self-doubt. Roger's wife described how their apparently equal division of labor has evolved:

> . . . with a lot of shouting and screaming on each of our parts. He's much better now than he was. In the beginning, I was in charge more, I was the one who noticed when the work was split or when it wasn't. I was the one who assigned duties, and I didn't want to do that. I didn't want to notice when we were out of milk, even though he would go get the milk. It's still uneven, but we have it more equal than any other couple I know.

An apparently crucial step in the change process is to tolerate inefficiency and ineffectiveness during the transitional stage. Hence, in contrast to Lynn, who felt that she needed to silence her grumbling because she was unhappy with how others shopped, Connie described her commitment to divide domestic tasks:

> I can remember he started going to the grocery store on Wednesday nights, and he would come home with not enough milk or rotten apples. And he would say, "I'm not doing it right." Or "If you don't like how I'm doing it, you do it." Or "We have no more milk left." And I would say, "Well, we'll have to wait till next week," because I knew my tendency would be to say, I do it better so I'll do it. And I was convinced that I was not going to the grocery store, and that he could become equally skilled at grocery shopping.

Resistance surfaces in many ways in the course of change. As implied in Connie's description of her efforts to get her husband to do the shopping, there are many secondary gains of incompetence. This appears to be true of both genders as they make initial forays into the other's traditional domain.

If domestic tasks are not divided along gender lines, how are they determined? A solution that many found satisfactory is what one woman referred to as "Darwinism of housework": "We sort out who likes to do what least. I have an aversion to dishes, he hates laundry." However, this may lead people quickly back to the traditional gender-typed division of labor. Men and women may find the traditional tasks to be more familiar and more likely to engender a sense of competence than the cross-gender chores. In addition, performing the roles of the opposite sex may pose a challenge to gender identity.

Gender-role socialization also may produce an investment in certain tasks and standards for performance. For example, to the extent that women notice or care more about neatness and cleanliness than men, women tend to retain responsibility for setting and maintaining standards of neatness in the home.[14] A woman in her mid-30s described:

> We would have disagreements about who would clean the house. [How would you work that out?] Well, unfortunately, we would let it go until one of us couldn't stand it, and that would usually be me. And then I'd do it. [How would you feel about it?] I'd resent it.

Both women and men commented that their homes were less clean than their (mother-tended) childhood homes, but only the women struggled with guilt over it.

Men Doing "Women's Work." One third of the men described that doing chores around the house was problematic for them. Resistance to household chores stems partly from the fact that they are by definition largely undesirable duties. Women's socialization generally led them to believe that household chores were an inevitable part of adult life. Men tended to assume that these tasks would be done for them, as they had been done for their fathers. A man in his early 40s pointed to the dissonance he experienced when his expectations were not realized:

> During the time of active feminism, Jill became more vocal about her desire for us to share more. I tried to help; I sort of saw her point. We did start to share. I was never very happy with it, and she knew it. Deep down I guess I really thought the woman's job was to take care of the house. That's the way I was brought up. I geared my life to find a career, which I don't really like but that I knew would pay well, to take care of the responsibilities of having a family. I didn't want to do that and then also these other things that I didn't want to do.

In addition to being undesirable, household tasks represent women's work. Several men said their sense of masculinity was challenged by

---

[14]The differential investment of women and men in domestic cleaning and cleanliness seems to be reflected in the finding that single women spend one to two hours per day more than single men on housework (Osmond & Martin, 1975).

their participation in household labor. It is important to note that the wife's demand for her husband to share household responsibilities often coincided with increased involvement in her career. Hence, the request that men participate in the running of the home was not an isolated event; it was integrally linked to women's efforts to increase symmetry outside of as well as within the home. Resistance to domestic work was high among men who found it difficult to support their wives' careers. Chris, a man in his upper-30s who felt threatened by his wife's successful career, described:

> My attitude could still get better—that is, my attitude about accepting the seriousness of her career and helping out with household chores. If anything caused a lot of arguments in this household, it was the housework. Having a housekeeper has helped a lot. It used to kill me on Saturday mornings when I'd be doing some chores around the house, and my brother-in-law would say things like, "Does your pantyhose have a run?" It's still not even, but we've gone from 95/5 to 60/40.

Subcultural factors have a marked influence on men's experiences of increased participation in housework and child care. Several men commented on the increasingly normative phenomenon of meeting other fathers at the day-care center or grocery store. However, when men felt aberrant in their participation at home, they often felt that their sense of masculinity was challenged. At least part of Chris' difficulties stemmed from his not knowing other men who shared domestic work with their wives. A man in his upper-30s described an earlier phase in which his work schedule had afforded him more time than his working wife to provide child care:

> At one point, we were living in a traditional neighborhood, and I felt uncomfortable with my househusband role. I think at least 60% of my feelings were a result of the environment. I recall when our oldest son started kindergarten, I walked him to school, and a neighbor was walking her child to school. We got about halfway there, and she asked me what I did about ironing. It was really uncomfortable.

Who's in Charge?   Regardless of the extent to which chores were divided or shared, balanced or lopsided, women usually remained "chief executives" of the home. The largest discrepancies between wives' and husbands' contributions emerged on executive tasks such as arranging for child care, making children's appointments, and giving directions to the housekeeper or babysitter. Couples had a variety of explanations for this situation. Many said that women were better at organizing, keeping track, worrying, and so on. Men universally accepted this arrangement, often acknowledging how it benefited or was easier for them. A man in his early 40s stated: "Carla is much better at worrying about things getting done concerning the kids, and then I often do them. But it probably is easier to do them than to worry about them." A man in his upper-30s described:

> I'm very good at clearly defined roles. Like I give the kids a bath. It's fun— we play and shampoo and splash, and then I deliver them clean and healthy into bed. What I'm not as good at is worrying about them, like should we change schools or who needs what appointment. So Sara takes care of that.

Women also recognized this pattern but showed varied reactions. A woman in her mid-30s accepted the executive responsibility:

> I'm the organizer. I just have a sense when the laundry needs to be done, but then George will take it out and put it in the dryer. It hasn't been a problem. It's evolved and it works. I guess we've made it work.

A woman in her upper-30s expressed more ambivalence over the role:

> Basically, I'm in charge of who's in charge, and sometimes that's annoying and sometimes it's not. So we split things 50/50, but I'm in charge of figuring that out.

One woman in her upper-30s gave an example of when her greater sense of responsibility felt disadvantageous:

> Both of us try to carry an extra load when the other gets very busy. But it's definitely easier for him: I pick up the load as soon as he seems busy; when I'm busy, he's slower to pick it up. It's like I need to point out to him that it's time for him to offer to help out.

It is hard to have true parity when one person shoulders the responsibility for thinking about the tasks that need to be attended to. The examples suggest that the differences are significant rather than trivial. Most spouses agreed that they do not split tasks evenly, and often the woman's role as "chief executive" comprised a major way in which an imbalance persisted. A man in his early 40s who shares a significant amount of child care and household work noted:

> I think the key to the dual-career marriage working is the sense of balance. We both thought that was necessary, so it's been there. It's

worked extremely well. . . . but Carol is a more responsible person than
I am, and the more responsible person in a family will end up doing more.

Women's executive responsibility for the home may make them more
likely to carry home into work. The carrying out of a task is less likely
to linger with someone in the way that planning tasks and carrying
responsibility for decisions about children's lives might.

This arrangement of women as family executives serves to preserve
the traditional allocation of home and children as women's responsibility. In many couples, women felt that they were backed into the
corner of either having to nag their husbands about helping more or
doing the tasks themselves. Again, women's concerns about nagging
surfaced in conjunction with their roles as gatekeepers of domestic life.
As long as women generate the list of what needs to be done, women
and men both will consider women as ultimately responsible for
overseeing the home. Although many couples shared the implementation of tasks, few described an equal ownership of executive responsibility (orchestrating what needs to be done).

Hiring Out: The Issue of Support Services.   The woman's addition
of a career role deletes no other roles from her roster and prompts her
husband to expand his repertoire of roles as well. A natural solution is
to find others who can take over some of the proliferating responsibilities. The issue of child care poses particular dilemmas and is addressed when the broader issues of children are examined in the next
chapter.

Consistent with the strong tendency for women to remain executives
of the family is their responsibility for hiring support services for home
and children.[15] About half the husbands described it as the wives'
choice whether or not to hire household help. This view derives from
the assumption that the home primarily remains the women's domain,
and therefore they should choose whether to hire household help or do
it themselves. In many couples, men felt that in giving their wives
permission to hire help, they were contributing their share to housework. If the wives desisted, then it was their responsibility to perform
the tasks. A man in his upper-30s described:

> The day I decided to stop doing child care and housework, I said to Joyce,
> "I can't do this anymore. I want you to hire a housekeeper." She refused

---

[15]An increasing concern among feminists is that women have been able to advance
themselves in the work world only by relying on an underclass of women to replace them
in the home. Hertz (1986) and others have argued that families are devising individual
solutions to the problem of combining work and family rather than forcing society and
the workplace to grapple with this issue.

to. I told her, "Don't come back at me and say I'm not helping." She did
a few times, and I reminded her. I'm not using my free time on this.

Even when the decision to hire a housekeeper or babysitter was
mutual, women typically carried the responsibility for hiring the help.
The interviewing and selection task was characterized by most as
formidable and unpleasant.

The dilemmas about how much and what kind of help to employ are
critical for most couples. Because society has changed little to accommodate working mothers, many families, despairing that they need "a
wife," try to hire one. Round-the-clock, live-in help comes closest to
replicating the functions of the traditional wife. However, the prospect
of a live-in housekeeper troubles many. Couples generally want to gain
all the services and functions of the wife, but they do not want the
complexities of another family member. Many project that they would
feel intruded on or ill at ease having a nonfamily member residing in
the intimate confines of the home. A woman in her early 30s reported:
"It would take me a long time to get over treating anyone in my house
as something other than a guest—which is, of course, totally counter-
productive for our purposes." For those couples who do opt for live-in
help, any such concerns seem mostly to be allayed. A man in his
upper-30s commented: "We worried that to have another adult in your
home would change the freedoms of your space. But the fear that it
would be awful didn't pan out."

Another dimension is the emotional drain that potentially derives
from the presence of another human life within the domestic quarters.
A woman in her early 40s deliberated:

> We've thought about having an *au pair*. But we decided that all we
> needed, to add the last straw, was to have a homesick French teenager
> here whining. You would need to put up with it, help them through it, and
> we have enough people's problems already.

Couples with live-in help corroborate these hesitations and fears,
describing a range of difficult situations that they have encountered.
Consistently it is the wife who contends with the problems, either
conflicts over the work or the helper's personal problems. One wife
exclaimed, "There are times I feel like I've just added another child to
the family who needs to be taken care of!" In tending to the extended
family of domestic employees, women are again fulfilling classic
expectations that it is their function to take care of the social and
emotional needs of family members.

Two kinds of expectations about domestic life also contribute to reluctance to hire household labor. First, for many, it does not fit with images of family life. This kind of concern takes different forms. For some, it pertains to the example that they want to set for their children. A woman in her early 40s described:

Hiring a full-time housekeeper would feel very artificial. The children should be involved and see their parents involved in running a house.

Some fear that a built-in babysitter would weaken family ties. They feel that the nuts-and-bolts functioning of the home may be crucial glue that holds the family together. A woman in her upper-30s stated:

We could resolve some things, like when both of us want to go back to the office at night, by having someone come live with us. But we feel that if we get into that, we figure maybe we won't ever be home.

A second way in which surrogate help runs counter to expectations relates to women's traditional performance of the household tasks. A recurrent theme for one third of the women is their ambivalence about hiring someone to perform their traditional responsibilities. If the jobs of home care and child care are still perceived as women's work, then some women continue to feel compelled to perform the tasks personally. A woman in her early 40s commented:

Part of my feeling depleted and tired is my own doing: If I'd been willing to hire help, the way many working women do, I would have felt less frazzled. I don't know what that's about. I guess it's some martyr-istic need to do those wifely and motherly duties.

A man in his upper-30s remarked on his wife's resistance to employing household help:

It would be fine with me if she hired a housekeeper. It's harder for *her* to have someone else do it. There's some sense that it's *her* house, and she should clean it.

Coupled with women's reluctance to hire substitutes at home is a concern that the surrogates would not be able to meet the women's own standards. This runs parallel to many women's doubts that they could tolerate their husbands' clumsy performances of chores. At issue here is the theme discussed earlier of the home as a reflection on and even extension of a woman. The conclusion that many women reach is, "I'd better do it myself." A woman in her upper-30s commented:

I'd love to give all the nasty responsibilities of the house to someone else.
But you'd need to deal with someone else's style of doing things, and
you'd have to tell them how. So you'd still need to organize everything.

Although the majority of men gave permission to their wives to hire
household help, about one quarter commented on having to adjust to
a less immaculate and a less well-run home than their mothers had
created. As discussed earlier, the fantasy of life being easier in marriage to a full-time homemaker emerged in many of the men's interviews. One man, who wanted his wife to remain home after her
maternity leave, made it clear to her that he would not tolerate
diminished standards in the home. His wife explained how she was "put
to the test":

When I decided to return to work after maternity leave, he didn't endorse
it. I wouldn't say it was an ultimatum, but he did say that it was contingent
on the house and family continuing to function as it had: a full meal each
night at dinner, the house clean, laundry done. There were a lot of
comments made in the beginning, like "Gee, I haven't seen this shirt in a
long time." His mother never worked, and he had been steeped in the
old—I hesitate to use the word macho—male mentality that he would be
the breadwinner, and the wife would tend to the children and household.

The corollary to the women's responsibility for household help is the
men's responsibility for hiring workers to attend to the outside of the
home (yard workers, painters, and construction workers). Of note is the
tendency of these workers to be male, so that the husbands relate to
male surrogates and the wives to female surrogates. Hence, even when
these dual-career spouses are not personally performing the traditional
chores, the traditional division of roles by gender is not challenged.

SUMMARY: THE WORK AND FAMILY SYSTEM

A consistent picture emerges of the domestic world in the two-career
family as complex, fast-paced, hectic, and strenuous. Although the
dual-career spouses rarely have a sense that there might be actual
solutions to these pressures, they almost invariably point to a need for
more time and more slack in the system. Hired support services
certainly can help, but the reality for most of the couples is that they
still live with the constant experience of having much to do. Do the
couples have *too* much to do? For the most part, these couples appear
to be managing well the multiple demands of home and work, and few
suggest that they would trade this lifestyle for the potentially less

demanding one-career arrangement. At the same time, some costs appear, such as the striking lack of personal and social time experienced by many couples.

The greatest challenges stem from the evolution of expectations and the resulting tensions of transition. Issues involved in the relative salience of work to men and family to women prove sensitive and complicated to negotiate, individually and as a couple. Such issues comprise the legacy of traditional expectations that couples either reproduce or rebel against. The most consistent solution to the dilemmas of how to fit two careers and a family into a household has a familiar ring: Women tend to shoulder more of the domestic work than men, and men tend to sustain more commitment to their careers than women. However, there are also currents of change. Approximately one third of the couples are engaged in a significant recalibration of these work and family assignments.

Chapter 5

Dual Careers and the Heart of Family Life

I think it tears me up more than it does him to miss something at the kids' school. There's something inside me—I hate to say guilt, because guilt is a waste of time. But it's an angst that doesn't go away, a question of are you screwing up your kids. Normally I would never ever bring up gender differences, but I am now persuaded that this may be a gender difference. Maybe because we women chose not to stay at home, we have to live with it, that it's going to be our fault.

—A physician in her early 40s

We have what I jokingly refer to as the tag-team approach to child care. If I'm going to be in the office on Sunday, then I'll look after the child on Saturday, so that Joyce can go into the office. Joyce and I rarely spend both days of a weekend together, very rarely. I guess we rarely spend *one* day of a weekend together. We are both so busy.

—A businessman in his early 30s

The worst thing about the dual-career family is that it's unknown territory, and it's unclear how much attention the child needs from his mother and/or father. And then the other issue is how much attention the mother needs from the father and the father needs from the mother, and how much dual careers are going to lead away from that. Even though there's no difference in how much time we have together compared with the traditional marriage where the husband is at work all day, somehow it feels different. I don't know if it is.

—An architect in his upper-30s

128

In 1950, Erik Erikson expanded on Freud's definition of *health* as the ability "to love and to work":

> It pays to ponder on this simple formula; it gets deeper as you think about it. For when Freud said "love," he meant *genital* love as well as genital *love*; when he said love *and* work, he meant a general work productiveness which would not preoccupy the individual to the extent that he loses his right or capacity to be a genital and loving being. (p. 264)

Does the high work commitment of the dual-career spouse impede the ability to be "a genital and loving being"? How do the work lives of the dual-career spouses affect the intimacy of their family lives? This chapter focuses on how dual careers influence the two relationships that lie at the heart of family life: relationships with children and the relationship between spouses.

In the last chapter, we asked how children affect the careers of husbands and wives. In the first half of this chapter, we turn that question around and consider how dual careers affect children. We examine how careers influence couples' decisions to have children and then explore the process of maternity leave as a transitional time in the dual-career family. Next, we focus on the role of child care in the dual-career family. Finally, we consider how the spouses think that their dual careers affect their children.

The second half of the chapter examines the impact of dual careers on the marital relationship. In addition, we examine the spouses' views of how their work lives affect their sexual relations, a dimension of dual-career marriage that has been largely overlooked in past research. Our consideration of the marital relationship includes a look at romance in the workplace, another issue that has not previously been explored.

DUAL CAREERS AND CHILDREN

The Decision to Have Children

Participants were asked if and how their own and their spouses' careers affected decisions to have children.

Timing of Children. Over half the couples felt that careers affected when they chose to have children. Women tended to feel their career was the major factor in the timing of children, whereas men were divided between viewing their spouse's career and both careers as influential.

Typically, when career factors influenced timing of children, the spouse spoke of wanting to be "established" before having children. These career agendas often were set against the biological clock and awareness of women's diminished fertility over time. A scientist in her mid-30s responded to the question of whether her career influenced timing of children:

> Absolutely. I knew I wanted a family from the time I was in high school. I very consciously made a decision to put that off and have a career. I knew that something might happen along the way that would make it harder to get pregnant and have a child, but I decided it was worth the risk.

People who delayed having children for career reasons frequently said they subsequently felt pressed by the biological clock and decided to have a child even though the timing remained inopportune. A man in his upper-30s reported:

> The delay of kids was influenced on my part by career, by my lack of success. I wanted to get career anxieties out of the way, but that turned out to be an idealized view of how it would work. There was, of course, the biological clock ticking away, and you don't want to be 50 when you have a kid anyway. So it came down to, if we're going to have a kid, this is the time, and career be damned.

People whose careers have not influenced timing of children often echoed this perception that careers were unlikely to provide good opportunities for childbearing. One woman, typical of many, declared, "There is simply no good time to have children."

Many spouses who felt that careers influenced timing of children depicted carefully planned and specifically scheduled pregnancies. One couple scheduled a birth during the summer between the woman's graduate education and her first job; had they not been successful in meeting their schedule for the pregnancy, they would have waited two more years. A woman in her upper-30s described how careers had influenced timing of a child:

> There were some issues that were fun, but not too serious. I had a meeting in Denmark, Stan wanted to go to England in May. So the question was how to have a child without missing these great things. Or long-range research plans. In the end, you just do it, and re-adjust your

schedule. You decide to have kids and not have major life traumas in that period, like going up for tenure or having to move.

The predominant theme is that pregnancy and childbirth are replete with unexpected, unplanned possibilities. The success of dual-career spouses often relies on careful scheduling and efficient management. Pregnancies refuse to submit to these schedules: There were numerous unplanned pregnancies among the couples, and the planned pregnancies more often than not resisted being produced on command. This can be humbling, can be taken in stride, or can feel frustrating. A woman in her mid-30s described:

We tried to have it coincide with the academic year, and then miscarried. And we decided to get pregnant again right away, which we did. So who cares if the child coincides with the academic year? The college will survive without me!

In many respects, the refusal of pregnancies to cooperate foreshadows, even prepares parents for, the reality of children. One woman responded to questions about timing of children by exclaiming, "Well, I got pregnant at exactly the wrong time career-wise, so does that count?" Women often recounted similar experiences of things with children occurring "at exactly the wrong time." As a mother remarked about the changes ushered in with childbirth, "It makes you a trifle more human to have the baby spit up on you as you get ready to walk into a meeting."

Number of Children. Only about one third of the couples indicated that careers affected the number of children they had. Spouses tended to feel that decisions about the number of children were based on both careers rather than one. A woman in her early 40s responded to the question of whether careers influenced the size of her family: "Absolutely. Two is our limit—and we always say that our careers are our third child, that we need to take care of them too."

When asked whether careers affected the number of children, spouses often replied in the negative and then amended their response. Couples appeared less conscious of the influence of their careers on the number of children than on the timing of children. A man in his upper-30s responded to the question of whether careers influenced the number of children: "No, not particularly. Well, I guess it was, yeah. We never talked about it in those terms, but it was important, more for her, to put a limit on it." It may be less emotionally charged to admit that careers affect timing of children than number; the issue of timing does not imply, as does the question of number, that people value their careers more than having additional children. Alternatively, it may be harder for people to estimate the effects of career on their decisions about size of family. Many participants considered the effects of career on number of children by asking themselves hypothetically whether more children would be desirable if they had fewer careers. A woman in her upper 30s commented: "That's hard to say. If I didn't have such an absorbing career, I might have more mental space for more children."

Timing and number of children are not isomorphic variables: Couples who timed their children for career reasons did not necessarily limit the number of children for career reasons. Almost half of the couples overlapped the two categories. But three quarters reported that careers influenced decisions about *either* timing or number of children (or both).

Maternity Leave as Transition

Maternity leave (especially for the first child) represents a significant turning point in the lives of the dual-career couples. For about half the women, maternity leave explicitly constituted a testing period for what balance of work and family would ensue.

Perhaps most dramatically, maternity leave is frequently the time when women assess whether they will take time off from their careers and become full-time mothers for a phase. This period often crystallizes decisions regarding the function of work in women's lives. A woman in her mid-30s articulated:

> I left for maternity leave not knowing if I'd go back, when, or whether full or part time. But I realized, even after having a great experience at home, well—after 2½ months, I wanted to go back, and I really wanted to go back full time. I realized then how important work was to me: my social contacts and interactions; my sense of self had to do with being in a world with other people, where you used the skills you'd been building for a lot of years.

Women expressed curiosity about what it would be like to be a round-the-clock housewife/mother. Women often spoke in terms of this being a "trial period," of wanting to "discover" what it would be like to stay home all day, as a woman in her early 40s reported:

> I took off four months. I decided I would be a housewife for the summer. That was conclusive proof that I did not want to be a full-time mother ever again. I went so bonkers. It was terrible.

Women often expressed fears of what kind of person they would become if they did not work outside the home. They perceived themselves as increasingly "moody," "needy," and "lost"; among the most common descriptions were allusions to "going crazy," "going off the deep end," and "going out of my mind." It should be remembered that these women were contending with a newborn infant during this period. Hence, their lives were disrupted and out of their own control for reasons other than their not being at work. Notably, however, their reports resembled those of a few women who had been out of work for brief periods other than following the birth of a child. This supports a view that at least some of the effects of maternity leave are related to the time off from work and not merely due to parenting a newborn infant. A woman who had no children below school age at home when she ended one job a few months before beginning the next described:

> I found out that I really liked to work and that I really like what I do. I like the structure of it. I enjoy figuring out what to do with myself, but it was nice to not have to do that all the time. I was frightened by the prospect of seven days of unstructured time. I worried that I would get into cleaning the house.

Other women (about one quarter) returned to work after maternity leave with reluctance and profound ambivalence. Some had not expected to feel such loss and separation. At this juncture, conflicted feelings about day care were often salient, and thoughts of reducing hours to part time arose. However, most characterized the return to work primarily as a period to get through, as a woman in her upper-30s described:

> It was initially very hard for me to go back to work. I was very bonded, and I enjoyed what was going on at home. So who wanted to go back to work? But I was also very appreciative to have a career to go back to, and I could tell that I would be a less effective parent if I were doing it full-time. So I just stuck that period out.

Some women described substantive shifts in their careers after having a child. A psychiatrist suspended her work with highly disturbed patients for a period, feeling that they were "too much like babies that needed to be taken care of." A businesswoman found that she was much less caught up in organizational politics, because she felt her "emotional energy was occupied" elsewhere. A physician changed focus away from severely ill children, "having known that I would burn out eventually there, but instead left when I had a child." These women did not depict difficulty performing their jobs but rather chose to make qualitative changes following the child's birth.

No man in the sample described a comparable career shift related to a new child. Men discussed supporting and encouraging their wives through the decisions regarding returning to work, but the decision was clearly seen as the woman's to make.

Child Care

Who to Hire?   Concerns that someone else may not be able to vacuum or dust as well as oneself pale in relation to questions about surrogate child care. The child-care dilemma rests precariously at the center of the dual-career family system. The quality and nature of child care is crucial to the dual-career parents. The issue that these couples grapple with is typically not whether to use surrogate care for the children, for very few spouses consider becoming full-time parents. Instead, questions center on whom to use and for how many hours per week. The issue remains a sensitive, charged, and often agonizing issue. A woman in her early 30s described:

> I'm sure I have lost more sleep over this issue [child care] than anything ever. She's been in excellent home care since four months, and now we're trying to decide about school. My worry has been about finding the right person, not that I wasn't her caretaker. I realize I miss her, and really notice it on Monday, but once I'm at work, I never worry whether she's okay.

A man in his upper-30s who is very involved in his child's care reported:

> We're in the process of discovering how much child care feels okay for us. Child care is a very big issue, very big. I'm not against child care, but it's a real concern.

These individuals are exposed to and highly interested in the emerging expert advice on child care. Many parents, especially women, discussed the gap between their intellectual knowledge about child care and their personal anxiety. A woman in her mid-30s described her first exposure to it:

> Child care was a real concern for me. I knew what our goal was, but Jack really helped me. I used his confidence to bolster mine—especially before I did it, and in the beginning. I believe in day care in theory, and had done all my reading, but it was really hard.

Many people admitted to a troubling ambiguity and uncertainty surrounding the issue of child care, especially over the long term. Frequent comments were "issues about day care are so confusing" and "there are no perfect answers." Professional metaphors on the topic were common and striking: "the data is inconclusive," "the jury is still out," and "only the opening chapters have been written on day care." To some extent, these scientific images of the definitive findings on day care reflect the popular media's as well as professional authorities' portrayal of the issue. At the same time, the use of this language by the dual-career parents may reflect their subjective concerns about the issue and their subsequent efforts to "objectify." A woman in her early 40s described "the ledger sheet" on child care:

> I don't know that anyone has an idea of what the ledger sheet will look like in the end. There are clearly liabilities: The kids just don't get enough of you, but on the other hand, they're proud and excited. I feel very uncertain about the balancing and the priorities. You weigh each thing as it comes, but hopefully you keep track of it. So if you miss the school assembly one time, you make sure not to the next time.

It is clear from the interviews that both men and women devote extensive thought to the issues of child care. In the complex market of individual and institutional options for child care, a key focus is how to select high-quality surrogates. A man in his upper-30s described: "We have very high standards for babysitters. They need to turn on the tape recorder, sing with the kids, make up games, etc." For the most part, people expressed high satisfaction at the quality of care, and many reported surprise at how well it had turned out. A woman in her mid-30s said: "I was surprised. People who get hired to take care of the baby—well, I chose carefully, of course—but they take great pride in their work. It's worked out a lot better than I'd imagined." Several people described innovations to improve the quality and continuity of care. One woman, for example, asked her full-time babysitter to keep a daily journal on the infant, tracking new foods he ate, meal times, sleep patterns, moods, and so on.

Although both men and women demonstrate concern about child care, the issue still tends to fall into women's domain. As discussed in the last chapter, women carry the meta-responsibility for children's lives: Men may perform child-care tasks, but women tend to orchestrate and organize their children's lives. For most women and men, these female responsibilities are consonant with expectations for motherhood. A woman in her early 30s reported:

I worry that she has a birthday present for the birthday party this Saturday, and that it's time for a shot at the doctor. All those things that "one's mother" does are things that *this* mother does.

Much as hiring household help is typically the women's job, so too is the major share of managing as well as worrying about child care arrangements. A woman in her early 30s described:

I think Bob worries about it much less than I do. He thinks our child-care person is terrific, but that there are scores of others like her in the New Haven area. Whereas I think that if she were run over by a car, my whole life would go up. He sees her as less critical to his life than I see her to mine. Which isn't all that surprising, because when it comes down to it, I still carry the primary responsibility for taking care of our child.

Hence, for the majority of couples in the sample, women retain the role of primary caretaker of children. As one man stated, "This is the way things are, the way things *still* are." A man in his upper-30s commented:

She is, overall, a more vigilant mother than I am a vigilant father. I think if the children had to choose, they would probably pick Laura. They would probably feel that she's more there for them. I'm there for them a lot, but on a daily basis, she spends a little more time with them and is less likely to be distracted. I think they consider her to be number one and me to be number one-and-a-half.

Men were often interested in and knowledgeable about their children's care, but in a secondhand way. Typically their wives both made the child-care arrangements and received the daily progress reports from the caregiver, and then discussed them with their husbands.

Emotional Dimensions of Child Care. If women feel that perhaps they should personally fulfill the traditional housework role in the family, their concerns about someone else performing mothering are far more emotionally charged. Women described multiple ways of trying to ensure that their children receive care of adequate quality. A woman in her upper-30s described:

I was worried about the influence that babysitters would have on her. So I worked it out that she would take two long naps during the day, and then I would stay up with her until 9:00 at night. Maybe that was a rationalization, but that's how we did it.

About one third of the women expressed fears that they would be replaced by and felt competitive toward their surrogate child-care providers. Many echoed the sentiments of one woman who "worried whether the kids would think the babysitter was their mom." A woman in her mid-30s described her son's child-care person: "We found this wonderful grandmotherly type. This was significant, because that way she wasn't competition for me, but was very experienced." A few men alluded to similar concerns. A man in his early 30s described: "The kids at my son's day-care center all call the woman who runs the place Mommy Two. If they called her Daddy Two, I think it would tug at me."

Earlier we observed that the grandparents (the parents of the dual-career spouses) feared the effects of surrogate child care until they could see that their grandchildren were healthy and developing normally. Similarly, the dual-career spouses, and wives in particular, spoke of the importance of their observations that their children appeared happy and healthy. Many described the earliest period of day care as a tense trial phase, with much riding on the outcome. A woman in her upper-30s described:

> I remember bringing Elizabeth to day care the first time, wondering if I'd be able to leave her, knowing how much I'd miss her. I left, and then came back in a while to breastfeed. She and the other kids all seemed so happy. So what was there to feel guilty about?

Maternal guilt certainly has received its share of air time in the lore of the working mother. Questions of guilt over child care arose spontaneously in about two thirds of the women's interviews, but only half of this group reported feeling guilty. Thus, about one third of the women felt guilty regarding the amount of time they spent away from their children. Few men in the sample said they felt guilty, but many commented on how guilt can be an issue for working mothers. Because the task of child care continues to be ascribed primarily to the woman, guilt over not having round-the-clock parental care is still a woman's issue.

When does guilt arise? Women do not appear to feel guilty simply because they are not providing full-time mothering. Although some women describe chronic guilt at being unavailable to their children throughout the day, maternal guilt is most likely to be precipitated when a child encounters a problem that the mother is not available to help with. A woman in her early 40s explained:

> As much as I know intellectually that my career is great for me and the family, I feel guilt over not being there when there's a problem or when

the kids really need me. I don't provide those motherly comforts that are supposed to be part of the picture of the ideal family.

In particular, if something major or even minor goes awry in the child's course of development, the window of guilt is opened. One woman, for example, discussed her feelings of guilt over the ear infections her infant developed during his early months in group home care:

I think I have felt guilty. The ear infections probably delayed his development a little bit, and I think, gee, maybe if I'd been home with him. . . . But the idea of being home constantly is a pretty hard concept for me to think about. I've worked a long time to have a career, so the idea of being home all day, every day is just so foreign to me. So I don't really think of it in that regard. I think of it as maybe I should've gotten a babysitter, or worked part time.

Another woman described guilt in relation to her son's school performance:

At times I feel guilty that I'm not spending enough time with Sammy. Like his teacher said to us, "He's really smart, but he doesn't know his letters and numbers." Maybe I should've spent time with him on Saturdays doing ABC's, instead of going back to the office.

Women who had planned and mastered ambitious career paths frequently spoke of having simultaneous concerns for their children's welfare and for their own well-being. Interestingly, guilt about not being a full-time mother is not an issue for the few women who worked primarily for financial reasons and do not view their careers as self-motivated options. It appears that women who elect to work are more compelled to imagine what their life might be like had they chosen to stay home. The key dimension that women appeal to in grappling with their potential guilt is the inviability of their being full-time mothers. A social scientist in her early 40s described:

I'm honest with myself in telling myself that I'm doing the best I can do. There are plenty of child-study people who say that it's very costly to not have mother or father around more. That's not an option for me. I would make a lousy full-time parent. But the kids could use a little more parenting, and that makes me feel badly.

Although guilt in working mothers is often headlined in both the popular press and scholarly literature, it is important to distinguish guilt from desire. Many women expressed a *wish* to have more time with their children without necessarily feeling *guilty* about their present arrangement. Both fathers and mothers addressed the importance of finding the right balance between work and family, but women tended to describe the balance as central to their emotional equilibrium. Again, it is apparent that finding a good fit of home and work is not merely a pragmatic challenge but also a question of achieving an external life structure that fulfills inner expectations and desires.

Effects of Dual Careers on Children

This is not a study designed to look at the effects of dual-career marriages on children, and the children of the couples in the sample were not studied directly. However, the dual-career spouses did discuss how their children viewed their dual careers and how they thought their dual careers affected their children.

Benefits. About half the dual-career spouses perceived their children as more independent than they would be if both parents did not work, and the spouses viewed this as a benefit of the dual-career family. A woman in her early 40s reported:

> My kids have become more independent. If I weren't working, I'd chauffeur them everywhere. This way they've figured out how to get from A to B on their own steam, and I think that's a strengthening factor.

Related to independence was a perception that children were more actively contributing to the home. A man in his early 40s commented:

> Over the years, we've trained the kids to share all the work around the house. They've had to get used to not having us there to do it for them. And I think that's been good for them.

A majority of the dual-career spouses felt the kind of example they were setting for their children was another strength. Two factors were salient for parents, reflecting the two primary ways they have expanded their traditional roles: career for women and increased involvement at home for men. A man in his upper-30s summarized: "It's all for the better for our daughter growing up—a mother who works and a father who helps take care of her." A woman described her children's awareness of and involvement in her career:

> They're very involved in what we do. They'll listen to my presentations. Our daughter packed me a sandwich the other day, and slipped a "good

luck" note in before putting it in my briefcase. So it's very exciting for them as well as for us. They love the stories I bring home from work.

Several participants felt that with two working parents, children were far more aware of the world of work and its possibilities. A woman in her mid-30s commented:

They think a lot more about what they want to be. They must be affected by us both having careers! There's a bulletin board at their school with a list of what the moms and dads do. It was interesting how equal the status is. It's great.

Women were particularly likely to comment on their children's aware-ness of their work. The dual-career wives tend to spend more time with their children than do the husbands, and much as women discuss their work with their husbands more than the reverse, mothers may share more about their work lives with their children than do fathers.

Several parents perceived the children's exposure to other care-takers as advantageous, commenting on the expanded number of role models and increased opportunities to interact with others. A number of participants likened the surrogate caretakers to an extended family.

The dual-career spouses described numerous ways in which they feel that they are better parents because of their dual careers. Not surpris-ingly, because men's careers represent the status quo, women are more likely to note ways they feel their careers enhance their abilities to parent. A woman in her upper-30s described:

Hopefully we are better parents because we have careers—in terms of the ideas we bring home, things we have worked out in our own personas that we bring home, ways of being. I think it's good for our daughter in terms of role models—two people who are successful and involved with ca-reers, and who love her.

This issue of increased emphasis on career was also perceived as a disadvantage, but less frequently. A few parents (all women) expressed concern about the pressures placed on their children to achieve and the potential overemphasis on career in a dual-career family. A woman in her mid-30s stated:

I hope it's not a big pressure for him to perform and do great at school with two lawyers as parents. I'd be happy with him doing whatever he wants when he grows up. I'd hate for him to be pressured by it.

In contending that their careers enhance their abilities to parent, many women presented their fantasies of what they would be like as round-the-clock mothers. One woman declared, "I couldn't possibly be a better mother if I were full time, because I'd go nuts!" (These fantasies echo the descriptions presented earlier of women's experiences of maternity leave.) A woman in her early 30s described:

> There's no doubt that I spend less time with my son than I would if I weren't so committed to my work. But what would I be like then? I know this sounds trite, but I think this way the time *is* quality time, because I'm not resenting it or wishing I were doing something with my life.

Several women believed that they felt less dependent on their children to fulfill their own needs and less resentful of the children's demands than they would if not employed. One woman stated, "If I didn't have a career, I'd probably need more from my kids, and I think that would not be a good thing."

Although noting the benefits of dual careers on their children, several participants also acknowledged limits to the influence they could render on their children. Cultural stereotypes and exposure to traditional expectations continue to pervade children's lives, regardless of the degree to which their parents are trying to model a nontraditional relationship. A woman sociologist in her upper-30s described:

> When we decided that I was going on for my doctorate, the kids were aged 4 and 5. And they could not understand this, because women were nurses. And they'd seen us and seen me work for 4 and 5 years! Which said to me, despite how you are with your kids, the rest of the world is different, and most of the time they're out with the rest of the world.

Costs. The dual-career spouses also recognize that having two employed parents alters many parameters of a child's life. At multiple levels, disadvantages of dual careers revolve around the diminished availability of working parents to their children. At a concrete level, for example, parents frequently identified that their children's choice of after-school activities was limited because the parents could not be chauffeurs. Of greater concern to the dual-career spouses were the reduced time and emotional energy that they devoted to the children. The issue of time with children was raised spontaneously by a majority of participants; it is clearly a point of thought if not concern in most dual-career marriages. A man in his upper-30s described:

> I hardly ever hear them say we're not spending enough time with them. I think they're proud of the careers. I think they've been deeply involved in

the process. They've seen the evolution take place, since we hadn't already arrived at our careers when they were born. [How about in your view?] I think there were times when she didn't spend enough time with them, and other times when I haven't. But for the most part, I think it's been fine.

About one third of the spouses observed that children expressed occasional resentment about the lack of parental time given to them. Parents of toddlers and young children (about ages 2-7) were especially likely to note this. A mother of a 5-year-old reported:

I think it puzzles him the way some kids go home at noon and he stays. About two years ago he went through a "I wanna stay home" stage. There wasn't much we could do. He likes his weekends; he calls them his "stay-at-home days."

The children's reactions to their parents' absence often are, reasonably enough, bound up with their feelings toward their surrogate caretaker. Children's connections to and engagement with their surrogate caretakers can buffer their wishes for more time with their parents. The father of a 4-year-old noted: "There are times she doesn't like to see Mommy go off to work. And times when she gets tired of the babysitter, and says so, says that she's bored." The mother of a 5 year-old, who spends his after-school hours at his grandmother's, described:

Sometimes he'll say, "Mom, why can't you stay home?" or "Why can't you be one of the teachers at nursery school?" But for the most part he's been very happy, and he misses my mother-in-law, and she him, if there's a long weekend or we're away on vacation.

In addition to the physical absence of parents during the work day, children need to contend with the spillover of their parents' work into family time. Much as spouses complain about each other's emotional absence even when physically present, so too may children dissent if parents remain distracted or emotionally affected by work after leaving the office. Men and women both commented on this issue. Typical comments were: "They don't like it when I'm overstressed or tired." "They notice if I'm in a fog. They'll say, Dad, pay attention." "It's not always quality time that I spend with them. Some days I'm just so beat after the day that I'm only half there." Given the ubiquitous nature of spillover of work to home noted in the last chapter, it seems inevitable that children's family lives are influenced by their parents' lives at work.

DUAL CAREERS AND MARITAL INTIMACY

Effects of Dual Careers on Marriage

Participants were asked what advantages and disadvantages having dual careers had brought to their marriage.

Benefits. Three quarters of participants said their marriage was aided by the self-fulfillment each spouse derived from pursuit of a career. They said each spouse enjoyed an independent source of self-esteem, and the marital relationship was presumed to benefit from the satisfaction of each partner. The spouses also perceived that they benefitted as a couple from the combined stimulation of each partner's work life. They gained, for example, an exchange of intellectual ideas, varied experiences, and new people met through each work setting. A woman in her mid-30s depicted: "The best thing is that you're both in a world that's stimulating, separate worlds. When you come together, there's something to offer." Interestingly, the advantages of the joint stimulation were cited more often by men than women. Perhaps this reflects that a wife expects her husband to have a career, but a husband is less likely to take his wife's career for granted. The husband's appreciation of the contributions of her career to the marriage may also relate to the fact that the couple's friendships were more likely to originate in her work setting than his.

Half the men and a few women also commented that they asked less of each other because both spouses were involved in careers. A man in his mid-30s described: '

> Her having something besides the family to focus on, a direction for her life, means she asks less of the marriage and less of me. So in some ways, her having a career allows me to have one. The stability of our relationship depends on each of us having something that is equally consuming.

This gender difference also may reflect the unquestioned expectation that the man would have a career. We have seen, however, how an asymmetrical investment in careers can become problematic, and we turn shortly to the potential costs of investing energy in careers rather than the marital relationship.

Balance and equality in the marital relationship is a perceived advantage of the two careers. Half the women and one quarter of the men mentioned equality as a positive outcome of the dual careers. Women may be more appreciative of this benefit given that, in a traditional one-career marriage, the wife was the "one-down" spouse. A woman in her early 30s stated:

> One thing that is very, very important is that you're equal. You both come home after very full days, and both pitch in. And it's economic equality as well. I think that plays a major role in terms of your place in society and how you feel about yourself in your marriage.

Those men who highlighted equality as an advantage of the dual-career marriage were the most likely to express an ideological commitment to nontraditional gender relations. A man in his mid-30s described:

> Dual careers means greater equality between the sexes and a diminishment of a kind of master-slave relationship. I can't envision being with a woman on an intimate basis except as an equal. That doesn't mean you won't be fighting about who does what at home, and I certainly drag my heels along traditional male lines at times. But I want to share my life with someone who is not dependent on me, emotionally, professionally and socially. I want to share my life with someone who has a life of her own.

Costs.   The feeling that there is too much to get done is a universal difficulty in the dual-career marriage, leading to the nearly unanimous lament of "We need a wife!" Spouses often wondered whether the hectic pace and constant pressures of managing two careers and a family took a toll on their marriage. A man in his mid-30s explained:

> The careers drive themselves. They have a speed at which they travel most efficiently or most naturally. And that speed is a little fast for both of us. If there were a way to turn down the throttle a little, that would be better for us, but the conflict is how to do that without interfering with the career.

High work commitment affects the marriage in two major ways. The first involves tugs between the worlds of work and family; the second entails allocation of time within the family sphere.

In the last chapter, we explored the conflicts that arise between work and family and the possible implications that they carry for marital relations. We saw that one source of marital distress stems from one spouse being more committed to work than the other would like. For these couples, tension arises because one spouse seems "married to the job." A woman in her upper-30s commented:

> It often feels like he's more committed to his research, his work, and his career than to here, his family. It almost feels like time at home and time

with me is time taken away from that. It almost feels like he's doing me
a favor by staying home on Saturdays rather than going into work.

Importantly, spouses who appear to be grappling openly with these
issues in their relationship and effecting gradual changes evidence
conflict but not necessarily reduced marital satisfaction. In constrast,
spouses who seem resigned to the situation often appear relatively less
satisfied with their marriages.

In addition to the strains of asymmetry, couples who describe
symmetrical commitments to work also perceive a negative impact of
high work involvement on the marriage. When *both* spouses are
married to the job, they may have little energy left for their marriage.
In a couple in which both spouses worked very long hours, the wife
reported:

> There's so much to get done during the day, work is so crazy and
> demanding. And I do find, having given a lot all day, I have less to give at
> home. Sure if there's a crisis situation at home, I can rise to it, but on a
> day-to-day basis, the toll is that there's some limit on your ability to give.
> It's like that phrase, "I gave at the office."

In the traditional marriage, one of the wife's responsibilities was to
provide emotional support as well as a happy home and hot dinner for
the husband at the end of the day. In the optimal dual-career situation,
each spouse could provide this nurturance for the other; in reality,
neither may be willing or able to. A woman in her early 40s depicted:

> There are days when we're both so tired, when we'd both like to be taken
> care of, when we'd both like to have dinner on the table. Those times are
> difficult. Sometimes energy is depleted all the way around.

An important part of the possible impact of dual careers on marriage
pertains to how time and energy are divided *within* the family domain.
Three quarters of the participants described a pattern of devoting the
time that is left over after work to the children. When asked about
disadvantages of dual careers, over half the women and one third of the
men indicated lack of time together as a problem. A woman in her
upper-30s described:

> I think there's a real problem with dual careers, and we're right in the
> middle of it. You spend an enormous amount of energy on your career,
> and then a lot on the kids, and there's not much left for each other. You're
> exhausted, or one of you is high and the other is low. So there aren't
> many contact points.

A businessman in his mid-30s reported: "We feel guilty if we don't spend our time with our son, so consequently we short-change the time for the two of us." Perhaps this pattern of making time with children a higher priority than time with spouse is also true of one-career marriages. However, the dual-career spouses clearly attributed the problem directly to their work commitments and their concern that children not be neglected because of the dual careers. An administrator in her early 30s stated:

> We definitely don't spend enough time with each other. Interestingly enough, we do spend the time with our daughter, because we jockey our schedules on the weekend or in the evenings so that we alternate who is working and who is with her. That way we each get to put in a lot of hours at work, and we each get to spend time with her. The thing is, when you add up our time at the end of the week, we haven't spent many hours with each other.

The spouses used language that suggests that although they consciously avoid neglect of the children, marital neglect is an unanticipated, even unnoticed result. Participants often recognized this pattern of minimal marital time only as they spoke in the course of the interviews. A scientist in his early 40s spoke of marital time being "sacrificed":

> I guess we are both trying to pack in a 30-hour day, and the thing that gets sacrificed most is our time together. I guess what I'm realizing is that we should probably plan more time to do things together.

His wife, a business executive, referred to the relationship as a "casualty" of their dual-career situation:

> We don't have a lot of time together. I think that's probably one of the unspoken real casualties of two careers—yourself and your marriage. I think you get so fixated on doing whatever you can for the kids that you figure the grown-ups can take care of themselves. And I'm not sure that's true, or that they ought to.

Some couples who recognized how little time they spend together realized that significant energy is required to arrange more time. A physician in his upper-30s described:

> It seems like we spend a lot of time figuring out how to save time or make time. It's hard to budget time for ourselves. Maryann is my best friend,

and we used to have a lot of time together. Now we're trying to figure out ways to protect that time.

In the context of little marital time and of high pressure to attend to the needs of work and family, the managerial aspects of domestic life often take precedence over the emotional dimensions of the relationship. A woman in her early 40s articulated:

I hesitate to use the analogy, but right now I feel we are more business partners than husband and wife. It's like we operate this small corporation together, but the intimate aspect is lacking somewhat.

In short, for many dual-career couples, marital intimacy appears to be at risk. A woman in her mid-30s discussed:

I know that I've glorified the independence of dual careers, with both of us on the fast track. Probably the worst part is the lack of intimacy. There are such time constraints, and so little time to be relaxed together, to share in a rested way. You might even say it's surprising that we're still together, given that we spend so much time separate. Real love, well—I think that requires time and sharing.

As noted, women are more likely than men to perceive lack of marital time as a problem. A number of interpretations are possible. Women may have higher needs than men for intimacy and for time together. Given that women more than men tend to accommodate their careers to children, women may feel that they would still be spending adequate time with their children if time spent with spouse were increased. Couples in which either spouse spoke strongly about lack of marital time and intimacy tended to show some diminished satisfaction with their marriage.

Sexual Relations

How do the high-commitment careers of both spouses influence their sexual relationship? First we consider the marital sexual relationship, and then we explore the possible issues of romance in the workplace.

Marital Sex. Participants were asked to describe sexual relations in their marriage and in particular the impact of their work life on their sex life. Over three quarters of both men and women reported that their sex life was impeded by work. The most common pathway was that work precipitated a state such as fatigue, depression, emotional withdrawal, anxiety, or hyperactivity that then interfered with sexual intimacy.

Just under half of these couples reported that each spouse was equally prone to work-prompted disinterest in sex. These spouses described that work stress led to a lack of energy and concentration necessary for enjoyable sex. A man in his mid-30s described:

> Sexual intimacy is easiest when jobs are going along smoothly, like on a plateau. Like we have sex on weekend afternoons now, when I can get my mind clear of the job and concentrate.

It appears that marital sexual relations are interfered with not only by occasional work problems but also by chronic work-induced stress. Most frequently, people reported that work produced fatigue and energy depletion. However, a number of participants also experienced distraction due to nervous energy and elevated adrenaline. A man in his upper-30s described:

> The largest effect is fatigue. That gets to both of us. But that's not the only issue—I also get a kind of hyperactivity. If I come flying in at 11:00, the last thing I'm interested in is sex. I don't even "land" until 1:00 a.m.

Spouses said their psychological involvement in work also affects sexual relations. A man in his early 40s responded that work definitely affected his sexual relationship with his wife; when asked how, he stated:

> I think our jobs are very psychologically demanding. Research puts a strong negative burden on people. Part of establishing the truth is being hypercritical of everything, and since you invest your persona, your ego in your work, you're very vulnerable all the time. I think that generates a lot of tension, and it takes a lot of strength.

Over half of the couples who reported that work affected sex perceived that work influenced the wife's desire for sex more than the husband's. A man in his upper-30s explained:

> The way I feel about it is when you're down, sex cheers you up, and when you're up, sex cheers you up. The way my wife feels about it is when you're up, sex is fun, but when you're not so up, it's not that much fun. So my ups and downs at work don't affect my interest in sex, whereas her downs at work make her less interested in sex.

Men in these couples did not deny that work difficulties might affect their mood, but they found themselves still available for sexual intimacy. A man in his early 30s described:

> Both of us are less likely to be responsive to the other when under pressure, but I tend to work it out earlier in the evening. I'm snappy and irritable when I first get home, but then by bedtime it's out of my system. She doesn't get rid of it so fast, and then doesn't want sex.

Many women in these couples felt that their ability to feel sexually close to their husband hinged on whether they were feeling emotionally close at a more basic level. A woman in her mid-30s reported:

> John brings work home in the evenings, so we have very little time together for just talking. I would need more of that in order to have more sexual intimacy, in order to be interested in sex more. Especially if you have something on your mind, you need to talk it over and get it out of your system, because otherwise it's there, distracting you. [Are you and John similar or dissimilar in this?] Well, it's a different degree. The optimum amount of talking is more for me, so there is an imbalance, and there's nothing you can do about it.

In addition, women and men both described that wives were more tired than their husbands by nighttime. Frequent descriptions were that "there isn't anything left" or "she is spent" by the end of the day. A woman in her early 30s responded:

> I'm always tired, and I really do feel that has an effect on sex. He doesn't see that at all. He sees sex as a diversion and release from being tired, whereas I look at it from a more negative point of view, that I'm so exhausted I have no interest.[16]

A theme that emerges from these descriptions is that spouses often differ in the extent to which sex serves as an antidote to, rather than a casualty of, stress. Men were more likely to use sex as an outlet for tensions. In rare instances, sex provided a primary way for a couple to relieve tensions and to close distance that developed from work and/or interpersonal difficulties. A woman described:

---

[16]One source of women's greater fatigue relative to their husbands may be their greater responsibility for domestic work. The descriptions of the combined first shift on the job and second shift at home (Hochschild, 1989) produce a compelling image of a physically and emotionally exhausting day.

> I think we have a very compatible, healthy sex life. I think it assists in bringing everything back to a very basic level. We can spin off into worries and so on, and when you come together, it's a feeling of releasing tension, of being very stable and rooted. Everything can be falling apart in the office, and yet you have a very close friend.

In addition, one quarter of the men and a few women reported increased desire for sex following positive events at work. A man in his mid-30s reported:

> I find that if business is good and I make a lot of money, it's very much an aphrodisiac. There is sexual stimulation for me from doing well. It feels very exciting to have success. You work to a climax in the business.

A strikingly common pattern for half of the couples is that husbands stay up later than wives. It is unclear to what extent this contributes to or results from asymmetrical sexual interest. As reported in the last chapter, many men desire more hours at work. They frequently described that staying up late to work was a way to compensate for their decreased time in the office. Not surprisingly, staggered bedtimes are not conducive to an active sex life. A woman in her early 30s described:

> Ken pushes himself to stay up late. He's so compulsive, goes over the details of a case, reads law journals. My problem is that once the kids are in bed, I'm exhausted, so I'll climb into bed with a magazine or book. I'm out in five minutes. If you want to have sex or cuddle, you need to get into bed at the same time.

Women often felt that their husbands did not understand their lack of energy for sex. A few husbands acknowledged that they had lacked empathy until they had experienced a similar effect. A man in his early 40s described:

> I might have put this differently a year ago. The last year has been hard for me. I've felt overwrought much of the time, so I've been less interested in sex. It's given me more insight into how Carla feels much of the time.

Are the dual-career spouses troubled by the impact their work lives have on their sexual relations? Tensions about frequency of sex clearly exist for half the couples. Where diminished sexual interest due to work stress was reported by women but not men, the husbands expressed a wish for increased frequency of sexual intercourse. In addition, one fifth of the women expressed a desire for more sexual intimacy. Their comments mirrored those of the men in the other couples, who felt more available for sex than their spouses. A woman in her early 30s described:

> Sex is our most significant issue, the only main argument in all these years of married life. I'd like a great deal more affection. It's clearly not an issue on vacations, so his work must have a big impact. How many times have we made love over the past few years on a week night? I can count them on one hand. So there's tension, fatigue—but I don't think it has to be that dramatic. [Do you notice an effect of your work life on your sexual interest?] Sure, when I'm under extreme stress, I'm less interested. But to be rather candid about it, beggars can't be choosers. So if I'm feeling stressed, I'm less likely to initiate and lay the groundwork, but I can still be responsive.

To what extent are the attributions of the dual-career spouses accurate that work per se is disrupting their sexual relations? It is striking that the majority of couples reach this conclusion. Being too tired or too stressed for sex because of work appears to be encoded as a common part of couples' beliefs about dual-career life. Spouses reported that their frequency of sexual intercourse was greater on weekends and especially on vacations. Many participants discussed the ways two career-oriented spouses can become distant from and perhaps overly independent of each other. One woman, for example, described how she sometimes experienced their lives as "separate orbits" that occasionally crossed paths. Although she valued their mutual independence, she wondered whether it was taking a high toll on emotional and physical closeness:

> I think sex is a tough issue. You wonder, what kind of sex life are you supposed to have, what do other people do. Clayton works lots of nights, and I work some and go to bed early. I can't remember the last time we had sex on a weeknight. I've decided that what's comfortable is what's comfortable for both of you. On the other hand, what's important is for you to come to certain points where you realize, gee, we really haven't been that close. I see sex—well, in the last interview you asked what are the drawbacks of the dual-career marriage. I said lack of intimacy. I think that just being relaxed and enjoying the sensual aspects of life . . . those moments are fewer and far between.

Children comprised the other dimension of the work-family system to which many spouses spontaneously attributed a diminished sex life. At a concrete level, many couples reported that having children nearby constricts sexual freedom in the bedroom. In addition, caring for children contributes to physical fatigue. A man in his early 40s reported:

> Maybe it's not fair to blame it so much on jobs as on kids. They wear you out, and the combination of kids and work, we're often too busy, or too tired. So kids have definitely had an impact.

At a more psychological level, spouses described a siphoning off of emotional intensity towards children. A father of a young child described:

> Things changed a lot with the child. It's had a real dampening effect on our sex life. It's not just how exhausted we are, but also the whole experience of loving a child, investing so much energy in him. There's just less energy for sex than before.

Romance in the Workplace.   The possibility of extramarital affairs certainly existed in the traditional marriage. Classic office affairs involved men and their secretaries; at home, wives encountered a variety of males in the context of domestic tasks (delivery and repair men, store personnel, neighbors, and so on). However, women's entry into careers has changed the landscape of workplace romance for both genders. Professional women and men relate and collaborate as peers and colleagues. Working closely with opposite-sex colleagues, superiors, and subordinates is increasingly common for most professionals. In many professional workplaces, the intensity of shared work experiences contributes to sexual interest among colleagues. Both men and women might fear that their spouse will feel attracted to a co-worker who shares the bond of common interests and professional passions in a way that the marital partners do not.

Participants were asked to what extent romance in the workplace was an issue for them and for their spouse. They were asked to specify whether they talked about these issues as a couple and in what ways. In addition, participants were asked about romantic interests outside of the work environment for themselves and their spouses.

Almost uniformly, the workplace was perceived to be *the* primary potential location for romantic possibilities, flirtations, and jealousies. Frequently, participants exclaimed things like, "If I'm not at work, I'm at home, so who has time anywhere else?" Over half of the spouses reported that they joked and teased each other about issues of romance in the workplace. Typically, participants responded that they experienced sexual overtones in the workplace, but that relationships rarely got more complicated than that. In a few instances, explicit sexual advances were made.

Women were more likely than men to worry about the spouse's potential romantic involvement with a co-worker. Over one third of the women reported feelings of jealousy toward the husbands' colleagues that were not reciprocated by their husbands' jealousy about the wives' colleagues. A woman in her mid-30s described:

> I think our marriage is very good, and I think he's happy too. But we do spend a lot of time at work, and when I'm feeling insecure about myself, I can't help but worry if he's working with an attractive woman. She can talk ideas with him, and all sorts of commonalities of interest that I can't.

Women's greater apprehension may be well grounded: Men were more likely than women to state that monogamy mattered more to their spouse than themselves and that an affair would not be "catastrophic" or "problematic," except that their wives vehemently opposed it. A woman described: "Joe is around attractive women all day. I feel very strongly about monogamy, Joe says he doesn't. So sometimes I kid him about it." Her husband, Joe, reported:

> Beth is more jealous, so I probably talk less about women in the office as a result. We don't talk about our opposite-sex friendships much with each other. I don't think it would be fruitful.

Although women reported more concern than men regarding their spouse's interest in opposite-sex colleagues, men and women seemed equally likely to have flirtations in the work environment. A woman reported: "There's a man I flirt with at work. It's fun, but I would never have an affair. Jim could more easily have an affair." Her husband responded:

> Relationships with women at work—it's all foreplay. She worries more about it than I do. She was very anxious when I thought about going into business with a very attractive woman. She feared where that might go. I'm monogamous, but less worried.

A particular focus of anxious teasing were business trips and, for the few for whom it was relevant, the long-distance commuter arrangement. A woman in her upper-30s commented: "We joke about it. We say things like, Oh, you'll have a lot of fun on those trips. The truth is, between the lines what we're saying is, Be careful. (laugh)" Her husband stated: "It's not a big issue. We'll joke about it. Like I'll say to her, Doesn't our youngest daughter look like your boss?"

Most men and women discussed sexual tensions in work relationships as inevitable, playful, and flattering. Several recognized more serious possibilities in them and discussed the challenges posed by working relationships that become laced with sexual feelings. A woman described:

> If you had asked me these questions even a year ago, I would have been oblivious to the concept. I've been shocked to discover that two people have had a romantic interest in me, people I work closely with. I also realized that I had feelings that I didn't appreciate in myself, and that I couldn't stay on the edge like this. I couldn't have my cake and eat it too. So that meant severing myself from a friend for a while. I talked about this with Ron [my husband] at only the most outside edges—very light teasing. I decided that having come to certain conclusions about myself, it wouldn't be very wise. Also, over time, I expect to have a relationship, a work friendship with this man, so it would be difficult to have Ron know about this all.

Although specific, graphic details were not requested from the participants, it appeared that husbands and wives were not fully aware of the extent to which workplace romance was active or threatening for their spouse.

Discussions of romance in the workplace suggested another potential advantage of spouses having careers in the same field. Because spouses can share the content of their work, they therefore may be less worried about that being an attraction of other colleagues. However, issues of workplace romance appeared comparable for couples in the same or different fields. It seems that, in contrast to the attributions made by spouses in different fields, the threat of sexual attraction among work colleagues is not reduced by sharing the same profession as one's spouse.

Trust about fidelity is a difficult issue if a marriage begins as an extramarital affair. Similarly, if a marriage begins as a romance in the workplace, does that make work-related romance more charged? The majority of spouses initially met in a work-oriented role and setting, one quarter through work and another one third through school. Several participants echoed one man's response to the inquiry about romance in the workplace: "Well, I met my wife at work! But since then, no more romance at work." A number of participants who had met their spouse at work commented on their firsthand knowledge of the potential for sexual innuendoes in the work setting. However, their concerns about workplace romance largely paralleled those of spouses who had met in a nonwork-related environment.

SUMMARY: DUAL CAREERS AND THE HEART OF FAMILY LIFE

The relationship of high work commitment to family life has been a relevant but relatively unresearched question about men for decades. With the advent of the dual-career marriage, the question becomes relevant for both spouses. This study offers some observations about the advantages and potential pitfalls for family life that arise when spouses pursue ambitious careers.

The spouses' perceptions of the advantages and disadvantages of dual careers for relationships with children are similar to the perceived costs and benefits for the marital relationship. The spouses have exciting, demanding, full lives outside of the home, and their feelings of satisfaction and fulfillment from work are believed to enhance their relationships with both spouse and children. As a result, spouses feel less need to find fulfillment and satisfaction within the family, either from children or spouse. Dual-career spouses spend a substantial portion of time in their separate work worlds and perceive autonomy and independence to be salient characteristics of their relationships with both children and spouses.

Spouses view these dimensions of dual-career family life as attractions but also potential costs. The spouses' concerns with both children and marriage center on issues of time. With children, the concern is whether the children have sufficient time with parents (that often translates into mother) to foster healthy development. Notably, the spouses do not discuss a concern that their dual careers threaten or encroach upon their *relationships* with the children so much as on the children's individual well-being and happiness. With respect to marriage, the lack of time that spouses have together produces a concern about the health of the relationship more than the health of the individuals.

The focus of most dual-career couples is on insuring that children gain sufficient attention from their parents. The dual-career couples are oriented, both psychologically and behaviorally, toward protecting time with their children. However, the high commitment of both spouses to career and children ultimately places severe constraints on energy and time available for the marital relationship. Marital intimacy, including sexual relations, emerges as a potential problem area of the work-family dual-career system. This seems noteworthy given that the couples in this study represent stable, intact, enduring marriages. The ways even these relatively healthy relationships appear stressed by the demands of dual-career family life may suggest some clues to the reportedly high rate of dual-career marital failures.

Chapter 6

A System in Transition

FROM THEN TO NOW

The first wave of researchers on dual-career couples assumed that many stresses felt by the couples resulted from the newness of the dual-career pattern. They predicted that the first generation of dual-career "pioneers," as Rapoport and Rapoport dubbed them in 1971, would create a slipstream into which later growing numbers of couples could glide more easily (Bebbington, 1973; Holmstrom, 1972; Rapoport & Rapoport, 1971). The current study explores the ways in which modern dual-career marriage challenges and replicates traditional gender relations in the family. Although the research does not afford precise and direct comparison with earlier studies, it enables us to consider in broad strokes how today's dual-career couples resemble and differ from their predecessors.

Contemporary dual-career spouses do not see themselves as deviant as did the early dual-career couples (Huser & Grant, 1978). With few exceptions, today's dual-career couples surround themselves with other dual-career couples. Current dual-career couples believe a well-educated woman would be out of step if she did *not* want to work outside the home.

However, even as the number of dual-career couples has multiplied since the early studies of this phenomenon, many of today's couples still consider themselves pioneers. There is a striking lack of change in societal structures that might facilitate dual-career marriage. Each family feels the need to create individual solutions to the dilemmas of combining two careers and a family under one roof. For example, participants felt they were reinventing the wheel each time they had to arrange child care. Few couples felt that they could look to clear precedents or role models for instruction or aid. As a result, the current generation of dual-career couples continues to feel it is blazing new trails rather than trodding established ones.[17]

General comparisons between earlier dual-career research participants and the current sample also suggest some important differences. One third of the current group engage in a significant degree of role sharing, whereas very few of the early couples did. Similarly, Gilbert (1985), in a study of dual-career husbands, found a notable increase in the number of role-sharing husbands compared to the initial samples. The current role-sharing couples are marked not only by a reduced discrepancy between domestic responsibilities of wives and husbands, but also an increased comparability in the perceived salience of wives' and husbands' careers.

In the dual-career couples studied in the early 1970s, few wives equaled or surpassed their husbands in earnings. In half of the current couples, the wives earn as much as or more than their husbands. Although sharing the provider role challenges traditional gender expectations, none of the predicted dire consequences occurred, at least in the present sample of couples. (Of course, the current study examines only intact dual-career marriages.)

Perhaps related to increasingly symmetrical incomes, half of the current dual-career couples, as opposed to practically none of the couples in the earlier studies, report issues of comparison and competition. Does this increase reflect a decreased tendency for women to "put a lid" (Rossi, 1965) on their aspirations? Women's careers, on the average, are keeping pace with their husbands' more than in the earlier

---

[17] Perhaps the generation of children who grow up in the current dual-career families will no longer feel like dual-career pioneers. However, without structural changes in society, couples probably will still feel compelled to create privatized solutions that tend to be difficult to negotiate and idiosyncratic. Many of the dual-career spouses described gratitude at finding just the right person for their child-care and/or housework needs and recognized that replacing that one person meant, in the words of one participant, "returning to square one every time."

Also relevant to consideration of the future marriages of the sons and daughters is the performance of domestic tasks by surrogates. In the dual-career households, women are typically hired to perform the traditionally female tasks of child care and housework, whereas men are employed to do male yardwork and home repairs. Thus, although the sons and daughters are not observing their own parents performing the traditional gender-typed work, the gender associations with the roles may remain.

cohort. Few of the current dual-career wives took more than a brief maternity leave after the birth of a child, in contrast to the typical career interruption of several years duration in the earlier cohort. Two decades of sociopolitical efforts in women's rights and affirmative action have facilitated the career paths of the current dual-career wives. Hence, comparison and competition are potentiated by the more equal career status of the current husbands and wives relative to their earlier counterparts.

Alternatively, it is not clear whether the current couples experience more feelings of competition and comparison or merely acknowledge and report these feelings more than earlier samples. Rice (1979) hypothesized that the earlier dual-career couples tended to deny conflict and competitive dynamics to reduce cognitive dissonance arising from the conflicting demands of work and family. These earlier dual-career couples met with considerable criticism in their social and familial circles, and they often felt a need to defend their choice of a then-unconventional lifestyle. Although such criticisms have not evaporated, dual-career couples today appear to feel considerably less need to defend themselves. It is possible, then, that they feel freer to experience and admit conflicts inherent to the lifestyle, including issues of comparison and competition.

At the same time as these significant shifts have occurred, there is considerable consistency over time to the solutions that couples create to the dilemmas of how to combine two careers and a family under one roof. These solutions typically embody the gender-linked pair of expectations that work is more primary to men than women, and that family is more primary to women than men. These solutions are often not created as a grand scheme for integrating work and family but rather evolve in gradual steps that on a day-to-day or week-to-week basis obscure larger trends and influences of gender. A decision for the husband to return to the office one night while the wife watches the children may seem inconsequential in the moment. However, this decision has the momentum of tradition to propel it and may be a path of least resistance. Such decisions often begin to set grooves that become increasingly deep over time. Many participants said they recognized larger patterns for the first time or with some fresh insight during the interview. The hectic pace of dual-career family life makes it easy for time to pass without analysis of the broader trends. Like a pointillist canvas, these behaviors at close range may seem random, whereas forms and images take shape when seen from even a few steps back.

Interestingly, subtle shifts appear to have occurred in the dual-career spouses' phenomenology of these enduring gender-linked patterns. In the current post feminist era, some spouses felt that they *should* have a more egalitarian marriage than they do and that gender-based expectations and behaviors are unacceptable. The persistence of gender-linked traditions therefore becomes a source of intrapersonal conflict and shame. Because some dual-career couples have allegedly achieved an egalitarian division of roles (especially as portrayed and glamorized in the media), many current couples perceive a role-sharing relationship as a possible ideal in a way that the earlier cohort did not.

THE FABRIC OF DUAL-CAREER LIFE

Rules of the Games of Work and Family

The dual-career marriage is predicated on the women's crossover into the traditionally male domain of professional work. To some extent, women appear to be playing by men's rules at work more than men are adopting women's rules in the family. In order to advance in their careers, women move beyond traditional legislative roles to assume executive-level functions. Unless one were to claim that biological differences explain men's incapacity to manage the home, there is no reason to expect that men could not move from legislative to executive functions in the home. Much as men manage their corporations and research laboratories at work, so might they be expected to gain competence at overseeing children's appointments and instructions for the housekeeper—if women are willing to share that role.

This asymmetrical foray into the opposite gender's domain can be conceptualized in terms of power dynamics: Women are entering the male domain of power (work), whereas men do not increase their power in the family by performing and managing domestic chores. Burke and Weir (1976) observed that, in comparison to women, men experience participation in the dual-career marriage as a greater challenge to their sense of identity, because they are moving into lower rather than higher status work. Furthermore, and importantly, the current data suggest that most women experience their decision to pursue a career as a choice, whereas most men feel, at least initially, that they are pressured by their wives to increase their family role. The men who feel they choose to increase participation in the home—that is, those whose expectations change—appear to move most fully toward an egalitarian division of labor in the home and to feel best about their domestic involvement.[18]

But are women truly playing by men's rules in the male domain of work? It is striking how many dual-career wives reduce their work involvement to accommodate children. In order to understand the reluctance of many men to assume full parity in the family and of many women to match their husbands' work involvement, we return to the gender-linked pair of expectations and consider their implications for current dual-career marriages.

Identification of Self With Work: Men More Than Women

Both spouses in these dual-career marriages are pursuing careers that require extensive education and training and that demand tremendous effort, commitment, and skill. Clearly, work is an important component of the life structures of both wives and husbands in these couples. However, work carries differential meaning for the two genders in most of the dual-career couples. What are some of the ramifications of work being more salient for men than women?

The issue of comparative success reflects this differential salience of work. Because work is considered more central to the husband's sense of self than the wife's, spouses feel that it is easier for his career success to surpass hers than the reverse. Does the dual-career wife then intentionally de-escalate her career (Epstein, 1986) to protect her husband's ego and/or to meet her own expectations about his career being more successful than hers? The risk of affiliative loss may be real for successful women (Hoffman, 1977). Does the dual-career wife feel she must limit her success in order to protect her marriage? The current data suggest an enduring feeling in most women that to surpass their husbands in occupational success would provoke marital unease as well as intrapersonal dissonance with expectations of both husbands and wives.

Similar logic prevails in couples who base decisions about geographic moves more heavily on the husband's career than the wife's: A perception of career as more central to his sense of self than hers leads both spouses to decide that his career should be aided by geographic moves when possible. Similarly, a view of the husband's career as

---

[18] The current data are consistent with previous survey research that documents that husbands of working wives do not show increased psychological distress if they participate more in household work (Ross et al., 1983) or child care (Kessler & McRae, 1982). Rather, a man's increased involvement in family work appears to reflect greater comfort with a dual-earner marriage.

tantamount to his sense of self makes it difficult for spouses to feel that they should accommodate their careers in equal proportions for children. On the average, women feel compelled to compromise their own careers for children more than they expect their husbands to. Men often resent their wives' expectation that their careers should bend to family needs. Hence, in multiple ways, the importance of career to men's sense of self underlies an iterative cycle that perpetuates his career as more salient than hers in the family.

This male emphasis on work carries both potential benefits and costs. Men's career paths suggest an early established, linear developmental trajectory. Compared to their wives, men often gain a head start on careers that may help solidify their careers as preeminent in their families. However, men also may feel less able than women to defer decisions about their career directions. Compared to men, women appear to feel less compulsion to choose a career path immediately, and women may enjoy the luxury of deferring graduate education until they are sure of their choices or of later changing career directions. Men may be at greater risk than women of prematurely defining their career identity in order to stave off the ambiguity and insecurity involved in identity formation, referred to by Erikson (1968) as *foreclosed identity*.

A related issue pertains to the provider role, classically ascribed to the male alone. Men appear to feel more burden and less choice than women about filling the primary provider role, despite their wives' income. However, men also reap satisfaction from meeting essential needs of the family. In contrast, women generally feel more options than men about earning money, which may allow them greater flexibility in career decisions. Women's incomes, however, are often perceived as less crucial and more optional to the family, a view that can serve to reduce women's power in the family.[19]

Identification of Self With Family: Women More Than Men

All of the dimensions just explored—comparative success, geographic moves, accommodation of career to children, career paths, and in-

---

[19] Women's frequent reference to the importance of knowing that they could provide for themselves and their children if necessary both challenges and highlights the view of their incomes as optional. On the one hand, in the current era of high divorce rates, women feel a need to know that they can be family providers, and this recognition leads them to view their careers and incomes as serious and necessary. On the other hand, the dual-career wives speak of their ability to provide as a security in case something were to happen. They imply that their income and ability to provide would *really* matter only in the event that their husbands were no longer the family providers.

come—also need to be considered from the family side of the work-family equation. Is a wife's devotion of less time to career, compared to her husband's career commitment, a secondary effect of the woman's desire to spend more time with her family? Is the dual-career wife's fulfillment of her expectation that she will be more invested in family than her husband perhaps related to a wish to retain a traditional definition of femininity and/or a traditional source of female power? Or does the dual-career wife shoulder family responsibilities because she perceives a lack of options in the work-family system context of a husband who is disinterested in and/or resistant to assuming domestic responsibility? Does the dual-career wife fear that if she does not take care of the children, no one will? Is her reduced career commitment the only solution that she and her family can create to cope with the role strains of dual-career family life?

We find that each of these possibilities is relevant for some dual-career wives and that some trends are characteristic for a majority. Most women in the current study want to be involved in their children's lives and depict an approach-approach tug between career and family. At the same time, however, women continue to assume responsibility for many of the domestic tasks not solely because they choose to but also because they see no alternatives. The interdependence of work and family roles for men and women is paramount and is expressed in a dynamic cycle that characterizes the interplay of work and family in dual-career marriage. A schematic sketch of a prototypical cycle might show the following progression:

> The husband experiences his work as very important to his sense of self, and as his early career development unfolds, he desires and feels compelled to use a large proportion of his discretionary time for work.[20] In the early stages of marriage, this high level of work commitment is relatively acceptable to his wife, who is also ambitious about and committed to her career. Once children are born, the possibility of two highly work-absorbed spouses becomes less feasible and less desirable. Both spouses agree that the children require time from a parent. The man experiences no diminished need to use discretionary time for work, whereas the wife's career aspirations now co-exist with a sense of the children's needs and her responsibilities for them. The wife petitions for more domestic participation from the husband, who makes some concessions, such as working at home in the evenings rather than returning to or staying late at the office. On balance, he continues to devote more

---

[20] Research shows that job satisfaction and discretionary time at work are correlated for men but not for women (Sekaran, 1983). A man feels less satisfied with his work, therefore, if his freedom to use discretionary time for work is constrained.

time to his work than she does to hers, which solidifies the greater salience of work in his life than hers and the greater salience of family in her life than his.

Many points in this cycle might serve as the initial trigger, and infinite variations exist. However, once the process begins, it tends to unfold in accordance with traditional gender-linked expectations, unless at least one spouse calls for its arrest.

The greater emphasis placed on family by women than men renders feeling successful at the family role a greater pressure for women than men. Women describe more acute conflicts between work and family. For example, not attending a child's school function generates more tension for women than men, and more women than men report spillover of family into work.[21]

At the same time, the greater importance of family to women than men carries benefits as well as costs. Being successful at the family role gives deep satisfaction and pleasure to the dual-career wives and is also a source of recognition from others. Dual-career wives feel that they have a back-up role in case their careers founder. Women take into account, as they assume that society does, that their success in career is modified by the extent of their family involvement. The prevailing view is that success for women is comprised of a sum of career and family in a way that it is not for men. By contrast, men feel that they receive relatively little credit for being involved fathers or role-sharing husbands. Their success is still disproportionately if not solely measured by success at work, both by themselves and by others. Hence, although dual-career wives carry the burden of responsibility for both career and family, they also appear to benefit more than men do from the combined sense of accomplishment and fulfillment.

Attention to the considerable strains involved in women's dual responsibilities too often obscures the possible advantages of the dual components of success for women. Nadelson and Eisenberg (1977), for example, pointed out the different connotations of *successful woman*

---

[21] This finding provides some support for Hall's (1972) observation that women have two simultaneous roles, whereas men have two sequential roles. However, the near universality for both men and women of spillover from work to home suggests that at home both spouses have simultaneous roles. Furthermore, the current data suggest that Pleck's (1977) hypothesis of an asymmetrically permeable boundary, with men experiencing spillover from work to home and women spillover from home to work, is only partially correct. Although it is found that women experience more carry-over from home to work than men, both genders bring work home with them. Compartmentalization that has been touted as a way to reduce role strain and role conflict (Goode, 1960; Johnson & Johnson, 1977; Poloma, 1972) bears little relationship to the reality of dual-career spouses' lives in general and dual-career wives' lives in particular.

and *successful man*: The adjective *successful*, when applied to women, encompasses both professional and familial components, whereas for men, it describes outstanding performance in the work role alone. The authors summarized, "The dual connotation (for women) underscores the double standard that is prevalent in our sexist society" (p. 1071). Perhaps the sexism resides not only in the dual definition of success for women but also in the monolithic definition of success for men.

Abandonment by the Wife

When thinking about the fabric of dual-career family life, one is struck by the couples' recurrent emphasis that they have no wife. It is as if *the wife* is the collection of duties that wives have performed traditionally, rather than a woman married to a husband.[22] "We need a wife" often serves as a short-hand description of the time pressures felt by all the couples. Each family faces the dilemmas of how to balance time between work and family spheres, how to complete the tasks of daily living within the time left over after work, and how to assign the husband's versus wife's time within the work-family system. For most dual-career couples, management of the home now involves orchestrating a support staff. And, for many couples, one is perhaps most struck by the fact that the wife continues, in her postwork hours, to be *the wife*, completing all the domestic duties that make up the second shift (Hochschild, 1989).

Although not typically implied in the "we need a wife" lament, the traditional wife/mother also provided the socioemotional glue of the family. Dual-career wives, on the average, continue to perform the major share of these duties. For example, they carry primary responsibility for overseeing the emotional as well as pragmatic dimensions of their children's lives. However, the dual-career husbands, to varying degrees, are more involved in child care than their fathers, and some dual-career husbands are participant co-parents who are highly active in their children's daily lives.

Part of the traditional wife's role was to provide emotional and domestic support for her husband so that he could leave the house each morning to earn a living. When the wife instead leaves the house each morning for her own workplace, how does the husband fare? The

---

[22] Whereas the dual-career couples complained that they lacked a wife, they never described absence of *a husband*. What would the parallel comment mean for a husband? Although "we need a husband" seems an unfamiliar phrase, "we could use a man around the house" implies a need for a handyman, a breadwinner, a male role model, or a protector.

tensions of transition emerge around this issue. Some men, for example, feel that their careers are impeded by the wives' expectations that
the husbands help with domestic work, which typically requires reduced work hours. Older men are especially likely to resent the
demand that they share "women's work," because they feel that they
are fulfilling their "end of the bargain" by earning an income. Implications of these resentments range from one man's complaint about not
having "real dinners," to another's contemplation of divorce when his
wife was highly absorbed in her career.

The traditional ways the wife/mother expressed caring for and taking
care of family members often revolved around domestic tasks (e.g.,
cooking a meal or doing the laundry *for* someone). Significant adjustment may be required both of men, who have been socialized to expect
these expressions of attention and affection from their wives, and of
women, who have been socialized to show they care by providing such
services. Similarly, a man traditionally expressed his feelings for and
investment in his wife and children by providing for them, whereas a
woman felt taken care of by the husband who bought her life's neces-
sities and luxuries. With both men and women performing both domestic caring for and financial providing for roles, the meanings and
processes of family communication are in considerable flux.

In the current sample, few spouses feel that the lack of a two-person
career (Papanek, 1973) proves problematic. Although it is important to
recognize that two-person career wives, who received neither pay nor
sufficient recognition for their work, may have been exploited, these
women also may have chosen to participate in their husbands' careers
rather than have no connection to the work world. In this way, the
two-person career may have served some of the wife's needs as well as
the husband's. An assumption of the two-person career literature is
that the husband's career relies on the wife's work and would falter
without it. The dual-career spouses' perceptions of few problems
involved in having two career persons rather than a two-person career
suggests that this may be a case where people mistook what is for what
needs to be.

Marital Life

Taken as a whole, these couples depict solid, relatively satisfying
marriages. Spouses describe feelings of vitality and engagement with
each other around career issues. They perceive many advantages of
having dual careers and enjoy the benefits of both spouses having
exciting, fulfilling work lives. At the same time, however, there is little
sense of romance in many of these marriages. A predominant focus of

the spouses' energies is managing resources to navigate the course of daily living. A theme running throughout the interviews with many participants is a concern about marital intimacy.

Many men perceive that a career wife is preferable to a full-time homemaker, because the career wife does not depend on her husband for all her needs. However, for some men, involvement in work may represent an avoidance of and defense against intimacy, and the dual-career marriage may become a vehicle of expression for difficulties in relating. (The complementary question for women, as raised earlier, is whether women's involvement in the family is an avoidance of career and ambition.) Many men feel that their needs for personal satisfaction are met by a higher ratio of work to family than is true for their wives. A substantial number of dual-career wives describe that their relational needs are not being satisfied by their work-involved husbands. Although the current study does not focus on parent-child relationships, it seems that often these women turn to their relationships with children to satisfy needs for connection and companionship.[23]

Perhaps the finding that women talk about their work with their spouses more than men do reflects a desire of women to use work in the service of intimacy. Women may experience more need than men to bring the spouse into their work world and to span the gulf that arises from spending many more hours per week at work separately than at home together. At the same time, it is important to note that the dual-career husbands tend to discuss their work at some length with their wives. This stands in contrast to Weiss' (1985) account of men in traditional marriages, who rarely discuss their work with their wives. The mutual involvement of dual-career husband and wife in the occupational world may facilitate marital discussions of men's as well as women's work.

In addition, it is inaccurate to conclude that all dual-career marriages

---

[23] Chodorow (1978) hypothesized that women want to mother because it meets their needs for intimacy that are inadequately met by men, who define themselves in terms of separation/ individuation. Chodorow argued that women's propensity to mother is directly related to their greater relational orientation. Within a psychoanalytic object-relations framework, she viewed this orientation as deriving from the female's experience of being mothered by the same-sex parent that underscores an experience of connection and identification. Because the male's initial bond is with the opposite-sex parent, he develops an early orientation toward separation and individuation. In critiquing Chodorow's theory, Lorber (1981) contended that women's continuing fulfillment of the primary parenting role results from social and historical factors, including the separation of work and family, the inequity of men's and women's incomes, and the ideology of *superior mothering*, that emphasizes the rewards of family life for women and renders them financially and emotionally dependent on a husband.

follow this schematized pattern of work-absorbed husband and intimacy-hungry wife. One third of the men report a wish for more marital time. Furthermore, the marital distance of some couples seems the mutual creation of two highly work-involved spouses. Although these spouses do not necessarily complain about an imbalance of work and family commitments, the diminished time and energy the spouses have to devote to each other takes a toll on marital intimacy.

The nearly universal perception that work lives hurt the marital sexual relationship seems noteworthy and deserves further study, as none of the earlier dual-career research examines sexual relationships. Two other pieces of research lend some support to these dual-career spouses' perceptions that the depletion of time and energy resulting from their demanding work-family combination leads to a diminished marital sex life. A study of Norwegian work-sharing couples, in which both spouses worked part time, reports improved sexual relations following their shift from full- to part-time work (Gronseth, cited in Rapoport & Rapoport, 1976). Poor (1972) reported that the implementation of a four-day work week produced an unanticipated increase in sexual activity, particularly on the couple's extra weekday morning at home while the children were at school. Hence, the scarcity of time and energy for each other both emotionally and sexually appears a challenge of dual-career marriage.

IMPLICATIONS OF THE STUDY

Implications for Generalizability and Future Research

To what extent is this small sample unique and idiosyncratic, and to what extent can we consider this cameo portrait of 20 couples representative of a far larger canvas of dual-career marriage? The dual-career couples in the current study span a wide spectrum: The sample contains, and each couple embodies to varying extents, both traditionalist and revolutionary approaches to gender roles and the work-family interface. The patterns found here largely corroborate, complement, and expand on other recent research on dual-career marriage. The ways current couples vary from the initial dual-career research participants seem informative and theoretically correct, rather than arbitrary or puzzling. In summary, the current group seems to paint a fair portrait of modern dual-career marriage.

However, there are many questions about dual-career marriage that cannot be answered by the current study and that deserve further investigation. For example, what are the challenges and solutions of dual-career marriage at different phases of the family life cycle? In addition, future research could address the variations of marital and family issues that result from different patterns of timing of children and career development. Understanding dual-career marriage would also be greatly enriched by examining the aspects of dual-career marriage that contribute to its dissolution. Given the reportedly high rate of divorce among professional women (Centra, 1975; Epstein, 1973; Rosow & Rose, 1972), it would be interesting to examine the kinds of issues that lead dual-career couples to separate and divorce and to compare various dimensions of work and family in married and divorced dual-career couples.

Hypotheses generated from the present descriptive research would now benefit from examination in a larger sample. For example, the findings suggest numerous dimensions of the work-family system that appear to relate to marital satisfaction. These variables include the amount of time a couple spends together, the degree to which spouses differ in their allocation of hours to work versus family, the satisfaction of each spouse with their own and their spouse's allocation of hours to work versus family, and the degree to which division of domestic labor is satisfactory to the individual. These variables have received relatively little attention in the quantitative research on satisfaction in dual-career marriage.

Finally, the multiple dimensions assessed in the current study need to be explored in marriages between nonprofessional working men and women. Do dual-career couples have much in common with their less well-educated and less financially privileged dual-worker peers? For example, how does the dual-career marriage of the woman executive resemble and differ from the dual-worker marriage of her secretary?

Previous research suggests that some similarities exist, in the sense that dual-worker couples too are struggling with revised work and family arrangements for men and women and with the dilemmas that ensue from combining two work lives and a family life. Lein (1974, cited in Rapoport & Rapoport, 1976) found many of the tensions and patterns depicted in the initial dual-career literature to be equally prevalent in a sample of dual-worker couples. Studying blue-collar and clerical workers, Crouter (1984) found that mothers experienced greater spill-over from family to work than fathers, a pattern similar to the present results. The gender-linked pair of expectations appears pervasive in dual-worker as in dual-career marriages. From her research on couples from a range of socioeconomic backgrounds, Rubin (1983) concluded that work is more important to men and relationships (family) are more important to women. Hence, along multiple dimensions, results obtained on the dual-career couples appear to resemble findings on nonprofessional dual-worker marriages.

However, the dilemmas of dual-worker couples and dual-career couples also have a different cast, and the solutions can be expected to vary considerably. As Hunt and Hunt (1977) observed, dual-career couples represent the liberation of one class of women made possible by the continued subjugation of another—the working-class women who are hired as surrogate wives. Unlike dual-career couples, the majority of dual-worker couples cannot solve their home management dilemmas by hiring surrogate care (Benenson, 1983). Workers with less substantial financial resources must rely more on familial and social supports than do dual-career families (Angrist, Lave, & Mickelsen, 1976). One study finds that, among couples who pay for child care, professional women pay almost twice as much per week for each preschooler as do clerical workers (Angrist, Lave, & Mickelsen, 1976).

Clinical Implications

The present research supports the growing literature that documents opportunities for satisfaction and well-being afforded by combining the roles of spouse, parent, and worker (see Crosby, 1987). At the same time, perched in complicated balance between tradition and change, dual-career marriage provides fertile ground for individual and marital distress. Awareness of the complicated and potentially troubled dynamics of dual-career marriage may be helpful to clinicians and couples. The current study illuminates a wide array of possible sources of difficulty, including: lack of dual-career role models, spouses' own ambivalence about the dual-career lifestyle as well as lingering disapproval from significant others, lack of time for marital intimacy, comparison and competition between spouses about their careers, and overload of and conflict between career and family roles. Some of the conflicts associated with dual-career marriage are intrapersonal and are amenable to individual psychotherapy, whereas others lie in the marital relationship and call for couples therapy.

Certain questions emerging from the study are clinically valuable in highlighting the intrapersonal and/or interpersonal distress associated with dual-career marriage. What balance of work and family do spouses expect for their own life structure and for their spouse's life structure? What vision of the couple's collective life structure does each spouse hold? How successful in career do spouses expect themselves and their spouses to be? How do spouses envision the division of work within the home (e.g., household chores and child care responsibilities) and outside the home (e.g., earning money and forming relationships)?

Difficulties appear most likely to arise at certain junctures in the course of career and family development. Decision points in careers often provoke anxiety and stress within the spouses and the couple. Certainly when one career falters, individual strain and marital tension often emerge; issues of comparison and competition are most troubling during these phases. However, even positive career changes potentiate difficulty. Career transitions frequently involve the possibility of geographic moves and hence engender stress about disrupting the other spouse's career as well as family life. Typically, choice points in career also highlight underlying questions about the balance of work and family and prompt a re-examination of individual and collective priorities within the couple. Family events like the birth of a child, illness of a family member, or family problem requiring special attention serve both to increase the work load and role demands of the spouses and to raise questions about expectations regarding family responsibilities.

In general, distress in dual-career couples can be traced to a gap between expectations and reality *within* spouses and/or discrepant expectations *between* the spouses. The clinical task is to illuminate the expectations (which are often not fully conscious) and their derivations and to work toward creating a collective life structure that more fully reflects the inner wishes, dreams, and needs of the individuals. When the distress reflects a discrepancy between the visions of the spouses, the challenge is to find ways of discussing conflicting expectations and to devise acceptable compromises.

Topics of manifest dissension in dual-career marriage may obscure the underlying roots of the problems. Couples' arguments often center on daily, concrete stresses such as the division of domestic tasks or work schedules. Indeed couples may need help in finding workable solutions to the concrete but extremely complicated challenges inherent to the dual-career lifestyle. However, daily management issues often resonate with deeper level questions, such as whose work is more important or who is ultimately responsible for family life. Many expectations, thoughts, and feelings about work and family life have deep roots of which spouses are not fully aware and therefore interfere unconsciously with efforts to create viable solutions to the rigorous demands of dual-career marriage. Other thoughts and feelings are more conscious but also not directly addressed because they are considered taboo (e.g., feelings of competitiveness toward one's spouse) or provoke shame (e.g., traditional gender-role expectations in spouses who aspire to a nontraditional egalitarian marriage). The

clinical task is to help individuals and couples uncover these underlying issues and enable them to be discussed in the marriage rather
than channelled into repetitive debates.

Importantly, conflict between dual-career spouses is often productive and ultimately may enhance marital satisfaction. Couples in the
study who achieved a relatively equitable and satisfying division of
roles describe considerable conflict en route to role sharing. The ability
to confront disappointments and to air grievances allows couples to
move toward their ideals and to tolerate the stresses inherent to their
complicated lives. In contrast, spouses who seem resigned to a wide
gap between their expectations and reality appear less satisfied with
their personal lives and their marriages.

Levinson and his colleagues (1978) described a life structure as
viable to the extent that it works in the world and *suitable* to the extent
that it reflects the needs and dreams of the self. A goal for therapy is to
create a life structure that is both suitable and viable (Howenstine,
Silberstein, Newton, & Newton, in press). The dual-career life structure
can be problematic in terms of either viability or suitability; the
therapeutic challenge is to facilitate a combination of work and family
life that is viable and manageable and also fits with the inner needs and
expectations of the spouses.

Dual-career couples often feel enormous pressure to perform. The
pervasive expectation is that they will be busy but happy: Their
professional careers reflect considerable achievement; they lead lives
of privilege; and their juggling of work and family is held up in modern
society as having it all. However, the formula that equates having it all
with happiness may make it difficult for dual-career spouses to acknowledge their distress in much the same way that many of their own
mothers were probably subject to "the feminine mystique" depicted by
Friedan (1963). Psychotherapy, as individuals or a couple, can clearly
facilitate locating the sources of distress in the dual-career system and
help create more satisfying solutions to the dilemmas it poses.

SWIMMING UPSTREAM: THE PROCESS OF CHANGE

People resist changing ingrained expectations, as revising expectations means battling personal history and societal precedent. When
change involves interpersonal as well as intrapersonal negotiation, the
costs and uncertainty seem especially daunting. However, as Thoits
(1987) argued, social scientists often mistakenly assume that roles are
fixed and that people are passive recipients of role ascriptions rather
than active participants in constructing their lives. Dual-career mar-

riage is testimony to the change that people are capable of effecting in themselves and in significant others.

It is important to recognize the heterogeneity that characterizes the roles and role expectations of the current sample of dual-career couples. We see great variation, for example, in couples' expectations at the outset of marriage, in their current division of domestic labor, and in the relative salience of the two careers. Some of the variance relates to the age span of this sample. However, the degree of heterogeneity evident in the sample also reflects the current transitional era. People's desire, willingness, and ability to change their roles varies enormously, and these couples represent a broad spectrum of solutions to the current dilemmas of gender relations and the work-family interface.

Comparing dual-career couples to their parents suggests that some current gender arrangements represent a significant revolution of work and family roles. In one third of the couples, husbands and wives share the major portion of child care and housework within the home, while both spouses pursue robust, continuous, high-commitment careers outside of the home. What differentiates them from the dual-career couples who have changed their roles less dramatically?

At the center of the change process lies the extent to which individuals continue to identify work as a largely male domain and family as a largely female arena. Men are more likely to share family roles if:

1. They are ideologically committed to equity in general and to shared domestic labor in particular. The importance of expectations supports Pleck's (1978) hypothesis that beliefs about the proper roles of men and women influence men's involvement in family work more than "reality factors" such as the amount of housework or child care that needs to be done. Other research corroborates the crucial function of role expectations in men's participation in domestic work (Baruch & Barnett, 1981; Bohen & Viveros-Long, 1981; Perucci, Potter, & Rhoads, 1978). The current dual-career husbands often combine an egalitarian ethic with a strong belief in the value of paternal involvement in child care. Similarly, Gilbert (1985) found that the degree of importance that fathers placed on being a parent related to their likelihood of participating in child care.

2. The men perceive their wives' careers as equally serious and important as their own. Other recent research corroborates the relationship between a man's participation in family work and his perceptions of high work commitment in his wife (Gilbert, 1985), in contrast to Bahr's (1974) observation that high work-committed women received less help from their husbands than low work-committed women.

3. The man is willing to expand his sense of identity beyond the work domain. The role-sharing men allow their identification with work and their view of its importance to be counterbalanced and tempered by an identification with family. A Swedish study finds that role-sharing husbands were relatively disinterested in work as a source of self-esteem (Haas, 1982b). The current study suggests that role sharing is aided not so much by a disinterest in work as by a willingness and ability to experience family as well as work as contributing to self-worth. These men show substantial investment of self in career but not to the exclusion of investment of self in family.

In counterpoint are the ingredients that cement men's alliance with tradition and enhance their resistance to change. One is a perception of the role changes as unfair, and a persistent belief in the correctness of traditional gender roles. This view is most prevalent among older husbands in the sample. The second factor that decreases men's likelihood of changing is a view of the wife's career as inherently less important, serious, or successful than their own. These men typically feel that the wife's work is "good for her" (a finding also noted by Weiss, 1985) but that her career should in no way affect or impede the husband's work. The third dimension is an unwavering devotion to work, entailing commitment of tremendous psychological energy and time. For these men, work comprises the core source of identity, and time devoted to family life is often weighed in terms of time away from work. This overriding commitment to work is observed equally among younger and older men in the sample.

The three components that increase the likelihood of change for women parallel the three factors just described for men:

1. A belief in the goal of role sharing seems crucial. Ideological commitment to the endeavor, often framed in terms of gender equality and women's rights, provides a buttress in the face of resistance, both from the husband and from within the woman herself.

2. Change is facilitated by women's belief that their careers are important, both on their own terms and relative to their husband's careers.

3. Women have to compromise their own standards at home and to share responsibility for tasks with which they have been socialized to identify.

Hence, whereas men face the challenge of loosening the equation of self with work and strengthening the identification of self with family, women confront the opposite task.

It is also important to consider the challenges of the change process itself. Women typically assume the role of initiating change, whereas men typically operate, behaviorally if not ideologically, to resist change and preserve tradition. Women thus require considerable tolerance for conflict. To incite conflict in the family is antithetical to the classic wife/mother role of family pacifist, who puts others' needs before her own. Yet, in order for women to persevere in the upstream process of revamping their own and their spouses' expectations, women need to tolerate a view of themselves as rocking rather than steadying the boat.

The iterative nature of the change process is a crucial dimension of the swim upstream. In role-sharing couples, neither husband nor wife alone is responsible for creating the nontraditional gender arrangements. Rather, the interaction between the two spouses, entailing small steps over a long time, results in the evolution of a new pattern of work and family roles.

Further movements towards parity in the dual-career marriage will require changes in the enduring corners of tradition that continue for most of these couples. If men contribute fully to domestic life and if geographic relocations are dictated by the wives' careers as often as by the husbands', can men and women alike tolerate the probable resultant reduction in the men's career success? If neither spouse makes greater career concessions to accommodate family, can women and men accept the likely outcome that the seesaw of success will tilt as frequently in her direction as in his?

This study dissects a system in transition. Dual-career marriages, presumably representing the more progressive end of the spectrum of gender roles in marriage, show both impressive innovation in and remarkable resistance to changing gender roles. Dual-career couples build life structures with one foot in the past, mimicking traditional marriages of their parents' generation, and one foot in the feminist-influenced present, making bold changes in gender roles that seemed unlikely even a generation ago.

Studying dual-career marriage means pursuing an elusive, moving target. It is a structure in constant metamorphosis not only within society at large but also within each marriage and spouse. Taken together, the seemingly insignificant decisions of daily life (Who will tend to our daughter's chicken pox today? Who will work late at the office tomorow?) either revolutionize or perpetuate the gender-based division of labor in marriage.

Appendix A:
Research Method

PARTICIPANTS

In order to attain a heterogeneous sample of professions across the designated age span, a network-sampling approach to subject recruitment was utilized. Rapoport and Rapoport (1976) noted that the principles of selection for intensive qualitative research are more like those used in the natural sciences (e.g., boring for geological specimens at strategically selected sites) or in linguistics (e.g., selecting good examples of a speech community) than of the experimental sciences, where probability sampling is crucial. Glaser and Strauss (1967) asserted that this strategic sampling approach is not only appropriate under certain conditions but preferable to random sampling.

A sample of 20 married couples between the ages of 32 and 42 with at least one child from the present marriage was sought for the study. Both spouses had active, professional careers. Students were excluded from the sample. Individuals from a diversity of careers were sought, and an effort was made to achieve an equal distribution of various careers across gender and across the age span.

A list of 14 contact individuals, themselves engaged in a diversity of occupations, was compiled from the investigator's professional and social network. The contact individuals were asked to nominate couples who met the selection criteria. Forty-two couples were nominated. No more than 2 couples nominated by a contact person were included in the sample. No couples known previously by the investigator were approached. In all, 24 couples were approached in order to obtain the sample of 20, yielding a positive response rate of 83%.

A significant number of couples nominated for the study had dual careers in which one spouse worked less than full time. A decision was made to include, as one fifth of the sample, couples in which one spouse worked less than full time but not less than two-thirds time. In 16 couples, both spouses worked full time; in 4 couples, one spouse (3 women and 1 man) worked part time.

The mean age of the women was 36.9 (SD = 2.7), and the mean age of the men was 37.6 (SD = 2.8). Relative to their wives, 8 husbands were older, 7 husbands were the same age, and 5 husbands were younger. The average length of marriage was 11 years, with a range of 4 to 21 years. The mean age at entry into the present marriage for the wives was 25.8 (SD = 4.6) and for the husbands was 27.3 (SD = 4.7). From the present marriage, 10 couples had one child; 7 couples had two children; and 3 couples had three children. The mean age of the youngest child was 4.8 (range: 1-16 years). Three women and two men in the sample had been previously married; both of the men and one of the women had children from the first marriage, all of whom lived with the participating couple on at least a half-time basis.

The participants were drawn from the fields of medicine, law, science, the humanities, the social sciences, business, government, the fine arts, education administration, architecture, and mental health. The sample consisted of 12 men and 12 women with doctoral level degrees (MD, PhD, JD), 2 men and 3 women with master's level degrees (MBA, MSW, M.Arch.), and 6 men and 5 women with bachelor's degrees. Relative to their wives, 16 husbands had comparable level degrees, 2 husbands had less advanced degrees, and 2 husbands had more advanced degrees. Residences and work sites of the participants were located between Boston and New York City and comprised a mix of urban and suburban settings.

The average income of the women was $38,000 (with a range from $18,000 to $85,000),[24] and the average income of the men was $56,000 (with a range from $20,000 to $120,000). Family income averaged $94,000 (with a range from $40,000 to $150,000). Relative to their wives, 5 husbands earned the same amount (within $4,000 of each other), 4 husbands earned less, and 11 husbands earned more.

---

[24] One participant was completing an advanced re-training fellowship, for which she received no salary, and was about to assume a staff position. She was excluded from the computations about salary.

PROCEDURE

Each participant was interviewed individually for two sessions of about two hours each. Within each couple, husband and wife interviews were scheduled alternately (e.g., husband interview 1, wife interview 1, husband interview 2, wife interview 2). Participants were offered a choice of setting for the interviews: Approximately equal proportions of interviews took place in participants' homes (45%) and offices (50%); a few interviews (5%) occurred at the investigator's office.

Participants were asked not to discuss the interviews with each other until after all four interviews with the couple were completed. Participants spontaneously described the abstention as challenging, but compliance with the request appeared to be good.

All participants were assured of confidentiality. This included a complicated form of confidentiality that entailed that material told to the interviewer by one spouse not be reflected back to the other spouse. In order to protect their anonymity, identifying information about participants has been disguised. All names have been changed, and particular occupational information has been transformed so as to include relevant details without revealing specific identities.

A Schedule for Interviews (see Appendix B) was developed to guide the interviews and was revised based on pilot testing. Questions explored many issues studied in the original qualitative research on dual-career marriage, previously unexamined issues relevant to dual-career marriage, and issues that have received attention in quantitative research but have not yet been studied with an in-depth interview methodology.

In the first interview, participants were asked to describe the course of their own careers, including decision points along the way and possible role models, and the course of their spouse's career. Questions probed perceptions of how each spouse had positively and/or negatively influenced the other's career. The interview inquired how family and friends viewed the dual-career marriage of the participant and whether other dual-career couples had served as role models. Participants were asked how their dual careers affected their children's lives and decisions about the timing and number of children. Questions examined how work affected home life and how home life influenced work and looked at how much the couple socialized with work colleagues of each spouse. Participants were asked how much and in what ways they discussed their work with their spouses. Finally, the process and outcome of decisions about the couple's geographic moves were examined.

In the second interview, participants were asked to consider how their own and their spouse's career success have been advantageous and/or problematic for the marriage. Questions addressed perceptions of career progress and success of the participant and the spouse and probed issues of competition and comparative success between the spouses. The participant was asked about the couple's finances and about comparative incomes. The interview inquired about the effects of the two spouses' worklives on their sexual relationship and about possible romantic involvements at work. In conclusion, participants were asked what aspects of their dual-career marriage they would like to change or improve and were invited to discuss any topics that they felt the interviews had overlooked.

Between interview sessions, participants completed a written questionnaire on division of chores within the household. Each person estimated the percentage of a variety of household chores performed by self, spouse, or someone else in the household. Results are presented in chapter 4.

The majority of interview questions were presented in the preoutlined sequence. However, the schedule was used flexibly to obtain full and rich understanding of the topics under inquiry. In particular, all responses were probed and pursued until the interviewer felt clear about the respondent's experiences and views. Interviews were tape recorded and transcribed.

The data from the interviews were analyzed in a qualitative and descriptive way. The analyses sought to organize, catalogue, and condense the interview material while preserving and conveying the rich complexities and variations of the issues under investigation. In order to achieve this dual purpose, a combination of descriptive coding categories and of verbatim quotations was utilized.

A challenge posed by any qualitative research project is how to minimize individual bias in soliciting stories from participants and in interpreting their material. In order to minimize this, safeguards were included in the study design. First, a male interviewer was hired to conduct interviews with 8 couples, a total of 32 interviews. Comparisons of the couples interviewed by the principal investigator and the male interviewer revealed no pattern of differences in the content of the interview data or the process of the interview sessions. Second, an independent rater, who did not know the purpose and background of the study, was hired. She listened to interview tapes from 4 couples (16 interviews) and coded a sample of 70 items from the interview. Inter-rater reliability was 97% overall and ranged from 94% to 99% per protocol.

Appendix B:
Schedule for Interviews

INTERVIEW 1

Family of Origin

I'm interested in knowing a little about your family of origin:

  How many children are in your family of origin?
  Where are you in the birth order?
  What do your siblings do?
  Were your parents together throughout your childhood?
  What did/do they do?

Current Family

  When did you meet your spouse? How old were you?
  When did you get married? (Is this a first marriage?)
  How many children do you have and how old are they?

Participant's Career Development

I want to know about the history of your career.

  When did you decide to have a career (in a generic sense)?
  When did you decide on *the* career you now have?

Were there role models who influenced your choices? Who and
    when?
How important was it to have *a* career? *This* career?
Describe the course of your career. (Take about 15 minutes to
    have participant highlight major turning points and junctures in
    the career path.)

How has your spouse viewed and influenced your career over the
course of its development?

How and when did your spouse facilitate your career?
How and when do you think your spouse impeded or interfered
    with your career development?
How did you work out the conflicts at the time?
How do you see them now, in hindsight?
How about now: How does your spouse facilitate/impede your
    career?

Spouse's Career Development

Tell me about your spouse's career history.

How important was it to you that your spouse have *a* career? *This*
    career?
How has the course of your spouse's career fit with yours? (Have
    participant highlight major junctures and turning points.)

How have you viewed and influenced your spouse's career over the
course of its development?

How and when did you facilitate your spouse's career?
How and when did you impede or interfere with your spouse's
    career?
How do you view and influence your spouse's career now?

Social and Familial Context

How have other people in your lives viewed your both having careers?

Your family? Your spouse's family? Friends?

How does your dual-career family seem similar to the family you grew
up in?

How is it different?

Have there been other dual-career couples who have influenced the way you think about or work out your own dual-career situation?

Children

What factors did you take into consideration when you first thought about having children?

> Was the timing of children influenced by your career? Your spouse's career?
> Was the number of children influenced by your career? Your spouse's career?

What effect do you think your dual-career marriage has had on your child(ren)?
Describe your child-care arrangements. How have they worked out for you?

Work/Family Interface

I'm interested in how your home life and job life fit together. Some people seem to take things that happen in the office home with them at night more than they bring things that happen at home into the office. For others, the opposite seems to be true.

> How is it for you?
> For troubles? For joys?
> How about for your spouse?

When you and your spouse are talking together, how much of the time is it about your career, how much of the time is it about your spouse's career, and how much about nonwork-related topics? Divide up 100 points among these three.

> When you talk about your career with your spouse, what kinds of things does it tend to be about (e.g., people in your office, the content of your work)?
> What about when you talk about your spouse's career? (If conversations about the two careers differ in terms of time or content:)
> Do you have a sense of why it's uneven?

When you and your spouse socialize with other people, how much is it with people from your job, your spouse's job, nonwork people? Divide up 100 points among these three.

(If uneven:) Do you have a sense of why it's uneven?

About what percentage of the couples with whom you socialize are dual-career couples?

Geographic Moves

Have you made any geographic moves for your career?

How was the decision made? How did it affect your spouse's career?

Have you made any geographic moves for your spouse's career?

How was the decision made? How did it affect your career?

How about in the future?

Do you anticipate making any moves for your career? For your spouse's career? How will the decision be made?

Advantages/Disadvantages of Dual-Career Marriage

What do you think are the advantages or best things about being in a dual-career marriage?

What do you think are the disadvantages or worst things about it?

INTERVIEW 2

I'm wondering if you had any reactions to or additional thoughts about our first interview. (Elicit responses, addenda, changes.)

Success and Marriage

How do you think your having an accomplished career has been a strength or asset in your marriage?
How do you think your having an accomplished career has been problematic in your marriage?

How do you think your spouse having an accomplished career has been a strength or asset in your marriage?

How do you think your spouse having an accomplished career has been problematic in your marriage?

Career Development

What are your career ambitions?

How do you see yourself in terms of your career and its development: Are you where you thought you might be by this point? further along? not as far as you would have hoped?

How about your spouse: Do you think your spouse is where she or he would like to be at this point? further along? not as far as she or he would have hoped?

Do you think you are successful?

How do you define success in your occupation?

Do you think your spouse is successful?

How do you define success in your spouse's occupation?

Comparative Success

Back when you were starting out in your career and marriage, did you ever think about which of you would be more successful?

It's often hard to say that one person's career is more successful than another's, but I'm interested in how you think it would be if your career were more successful than your spouse's.

How would it be for you?

How would it be for your spouse?

How would it be if your spouse's career were more successful than yours?

How would it be for your spouse?

How would it be for you?

Has this been an issue for you?

How do you deal with comparison and competition in your marriage?

If the seesaw of success were not evenly balanced between your two careers, would it be easier if it tilted one way rather than the other?

Satisfaction in Life

What aspect in your life has given you the most satisfaction?

(If not an accomplishment:) What accomplishment has given you
the most satisfaction?
(If not a professional accomplishment:) What professional accomplishment has given you the most satisfaction?

What accomplishment of your spouse has given you the most satisfaction?

(If not a professional accomplishment:) What professional accomplishment of your spouse has given you the most satisfaction?

Finances

I'd like to get a sense of your finances as a couple.

How much do you earn?
How much does your spouse earn?
How do you, as a couple, deal with finances (e.g., pooled, sepa-
rate; who covers what expenses)?
What are the tension points/conflicts around finances for you as a
couple?
How do you feel about your income relative to your spouse's?
How would it be if your incomes were reversed?

Sexual Relations

As much as you feel comfortable doing, tell me about your sex life and
in particular the impact of your work lives on your sexual relations.

What is the effect of ups and downs of your job on your sexual
intimacy?
What is the effect of ups and downs of your spouse's job on your
sexual intimacy?

To what extent is there romance in the workplace for you? Elsewhere?

How about for your spouse?
Do you talk about these kinds of issues as a couple?

Changes/Improvements

In working out your dual-career marriage, what aspects would you like to change or improve?

Are there any other aspects of your dual-career marriage that you feel I haven't focused on or probed into?

References

Angrist, S. S., Lave, J. R., & Mickelsen, R. (1976). How working mothers manage: Socioeconomic differences in work, child care and household tasks. *Social Science Quarterly, 56,* 631-637.

Astin, H. (1969). *The woman doctorate in America.* New York: Russell Sage.

Bahr, S. J. (1974). Effects on power and the division of labor in the family. In L. W. Hoffman & I. Nye (Eds.), *Working mothers* (pp. 167-185). San Francisco: Jossey-Bass.

Barnett, R. (1983, August). *Determinants of father participation in child care.* Paper presented at the annual meeting of the American Psychological Association, Anaheim, CA.

Baruch, G. K., & Barnett, R. C. (1981). Fathers' participation in the care of their preschool children. *Sex Roles, 7,* 1043-1055.

Baruch, G. K., Barnett, R. C., & Rivers, C. (1983). *Lifeprints: New patterns of love and work for today's women.* New York: Signet.

Bebbington, A. C. (1973). The function of stress in the establishment of the dual-career family. *Journal of Marriage and the Family, 35,* 530-537.

Benenson, H. (1983). Women's occupational and family achievement in the U. S. class system: A critique of the dual-career family analysis. *British Journal of Sociology, 35,* 19-41.

Berk, R., & Berk, S. F. (1979). *Labor and leisure at home: Content and organization of the household day.* Beverly Hills, CA: Sage.

Bohen, H. H., & Viveros-Long, A. (1981). *Balancing jobs and family life: Do flexible work schedules help?* Philadelphia, PA: Temple University Press.

Bowen, G. L., & Orthner, D. K. (1983). Sex-role congruency and marital quality. *Journal of Marriage and the Family, 45,* 223-233.

Bronfenbrenner, U., & Crouter, A. C. (1982). Work and family through time and space. In S. Kamerman & C. Hayes (Eds.), *Families that work: Children in a changing world* (pp. 39-83). Washington, DC: National Academy of Sciences.

Burke, R. J., & Weir, T. (1976). Relationship of wives' employment status to husband, wife, and pair satisfaction and performance. *Journal of Marriage and the Family, 38,* 279-287.

Centra, J. A. (1975) *Women, men, and the doctorate*. Princeton, NJ: Educational Testing Service.

Chodorow, N. (1978). *The reproduction of mothering: Psychoanalysis and the sociology of gender*. Berkeley: University of California Press.

Cole, J. R., & Zuckerman, H. (1987). Marriage, motherhood and research performance in science. *Scientific American, 256*, 119-125.

Coser, R. L., & Rokoff, G. (1971). Women in the occupational world: Social disruption and conflict. *Social Problems, 18*, 535-554.

Crosby, F. J. (1982). *Relative deprivation and working women*. New York: Oxford University Press.

Crosby, F. J. (Ed.). (1987). *Spouse, parent, and worker: On gender and multiple roles*. New Haven, CT: Yale University Press.

Crouter, A. C. (1984). Spillover from family to work: The neglected side of the work-family interface. *Human Relations, 37*, 425-442.

Duncan, P., & Perucci, C. C. (1976). Dual occupation families and migration. *American Sociological Review, 41*, 252-261.

Epstein, C. F. (1973). *Woman's place*. Berkeley: University of California Press.

Epstein, C. F. (1986). Family and career: Why women can "have it all." In C. Tavris (Ed.), *Every woman's emotional well-being* (pp. 90-108). Garden City, NY: Doubleday.

Epstein, C. F. (1987). Role strains and multiple successes. In F. J. Crosby (Ed.), *Spouse, parent, & worker: On gender and multiple roles* (pp. 23-35). New Haven, CT: Yale University Press.

Eriksen, J. A., Yancy, W. L., & Eriksen, E. P. (1979). The division of family roles. *Journal of Marriage and the Family, 41*, 303-313.

Erikson, E. H. (1950). *Childhood and society*. New York: Norton.

Erikson, E. H. (1968). *Identity: Youth and crisis*. New York: Norton.

Farkas, G. (1976). Education, wage rates, and the division of labor between husband and wife. *Journal of Marriage and the Family, 38*, 473-483.

Feldman, S. (1973). Impediment or stimulant? Marital status and graduate education. *American Journal of Sociology, 73*, 982-994.

Ferber, M., & Huber, J. (1979). Husbands, wives, and careers. *Journal of Marriage and the Family, 41*, 315-325.

Friedan, B. (1963). *The feminine mystique*. New York: Dell.

Garland, T. N. (1972). The better half: The male in the dual-career professional family. In C. Safilios-Rothschild (Ed.), *Toward a sociology of women* (pp. 199-215). Lexington, MA: Xerox.

Gerstel, N., & Gross, H. (1984). *Commuter marriage*. New York: Guilford Press.

Gilbert, L. A. (1985). *Men in dual-career families: Current realities and future prospects*. Hillsdale, NJ: Lawrence Erlbaum Associates.

Glaser, B. G., & Strauss, A. L. (1967). *The discovery of grounded theory: Strategies for qualitative research*. Chicago: Aldine.

Goode, W. (1960). A theory of role strain. *American Sociological Review, 25*, 483-499.

Gove, W. R., & Geerken, M. R. (1977). The effect of children and employment on the mental health of married men and women. *Social Focus, 56*, 66-76.

Gove, W. R., & Zeiss, C. (1987). Multiple roles and happiness. In F. J. Crosby (Ed.), *Spouse, parent, worker: On gender and multiple roles* (pp. 125-137). New Haven, CT: Yale University Press.

Gray, J. D. (1983). The married professional woman: An examination of her role conflicts and coping strategies. *Psychology of Women Quarterly, 7*, 235-243.

Gray-Little, B., & Burks, N. (1983). Power and satisfaction in marriage: A review and critique. *Psychological Bulletin, 93*, 513-538.

Haas, L. (1982a). Parental sharing of childcare tasks in Sweden. *Journal of Family Issues, 3*, 389-412.

Haas, L. (1982b). Determinants of role-sharing behavior: A study of egalitarian couples. *Sex Roles, 8*, 747-760.

Hall, D. T. (1972). A model of coping with role conflict: The role behavior of college-educated women. *Administrative Science Quarterly, 17*, 471-486.

Hardesty, S. A., & Betz, N. A. (1980). The relationships of career salience, attitudes toward women, and demographic and family characteristics to marital adjustment in dual-career couples. *Journal of Vocational Behavior, 17*, 242-250.

Havens, E. M. (1973). Women, work, and wedlock: A note on female marital patterns in the United States. *American Journal of Sociology, 78*, 975-981.

Heckman, N. A., Bryson, R., & Bryson, J. B. (1977). Problems of professional couples: A content analysis. *Journal of Marriage and the Family, 39*, 323-330.

Hertz, R. (1986). *More equal than others: Women and men in dual-career marriages.* Berkeley: University of California Press.

Hochschild, A. (1989). *The second shift: Working parents and the revolution at home.* New York: Viking.

Hoffman, L. W. (1977). Changes in family roles, socialization, and sex differences. *American Psychologist, 32*, 644-657.

Hoffman, L. W. (1985). Preface. In L. A. Gilbert, *Men in dual-career families: Current realities and future prospects.* Hillsdale, NJ: Lawrence Erlbaum Associates.

Holmstrom, L. L. (1972). *The two-career family.* Cambridge, MA: Schenkman.

Hornung, C. A., & McCullough, B. C. (1981). Status relationships in dual-employment marriage: Consequences for psychological well-being. *Journal of Marriage and the Family, 43*, 125-142.

Houseknecht, S. K., & Spanier, G. B. (1980). Marital disruption and higher education among women in the United States. *The Sociological Quarterly, 21*, 375-389.

Howenstine, R.A., Silberstein, L.R., Newton, D.S., & Newton, P.M. (in press). Life structure revitalization: An adult development approach to psychodynamic psychotherapy. *Psychiatry.*

Hunt, J. G., & Hunt, L. L. (1977). Dilemmas and contradictions of status: The case of the dual-career family. *Social Problems, 24*, 407-416.

Huser, W. R., & Grant, C. W. (1978). A study of husbands and wives from dual-career and traditional-career families. *Psychology of Women Quarterly, 3*, 78-89.

Jacoby, R. (1975). *Social amnesia.* Boston: Beacon Press.

Johnson, C. L., & Johnson, F. A. (1977). Attitudes toward parenting in dual-career families. *American Journal of Psychiatry, 134*, 391-395.

Johnson, F. A., & Johnson, C. L. (1976). Role strains in high commitment career women. *Journal of the American Academy of Psychoanalysis, 4*, 37-48.

Kanter, R. M. (1977). *Work and family in the United States: A critical review and agenda for research and policy.* New York: Russell Sage Foundation.

Kaufman, D. (1978). Associational ties in academe: Some male and female differences. *Sex Roles, 4*, 9-12.

Kelley, H. H. (1979). *Personal relationships: Their structure and power.* New York: Halstead.

Kessler, R. C., & McRae, J. A. (1981). Trends in the relationship between sex and psychological distress: 1957-1976. *American Sociological Review, 46*, 443-452.

Kessler, R. C., & McRae, J. A. (1982). The effect of wives' employment on the mental health of married men and women. *American Sociological Review, 47*, 216-227.

Lave, J. R., & Angrist, S. S. (1975). Childcare arrangements of working mothers: Social and economic aspects. *International Journal of Sociology of the Family, 5*, 230–232.

Levinson, D. J., with Darrow, C. M., Klein, E. B., Levinson, M.H., & McKee, B. (1978). *The seasons of a man's life*. New York: Knopf.

Lewis, R. A., & Spanier, G. B. (1979). Theorizing about the quality and stability of marriage. In W. R. Burr, R. Hill, F. I. Nye, & I. L. Reiss (Eds.), *Contemporary theories about the family* (Vol. 1, pp. 268-294). New York: The Free Press.

Lorber, J. (1981). On *The reproduction of mothering*: A methodological debate. *Signs, 6,* 482-486.

Lynn, D. B. (1980). Intellectual development of women. In F. Pepitone-Rockwell (Ed.), *Dual-career couples* (pp. 55-71). Beverly Hills: Sage.

Mamay, P. D., & Simpson, R. L. (1981). Three female roles in television commercials. *Sex Roles, 7,* 1223-1232.

Meissner, M., Humphreys, E. W., Meis, S. M., & Scheu, M. J. (1975). No exit for wives: Sexual division of labor and the cumulation of household demands. *Canadian Review of Sociology and Anthropology, 12,* 424-439.

Model, S. (1982). Housework by husbands: Determinants and implications. In J. Aldous (Ed.), *Two paychecks: Life in dual-earner families* (pp. 193-205). Beverly Hills, CA: Sage.

Mueller, C. W., & Campbell, B. G. (1977). Female occupational achievement and marital status: A research note. *Journal of Marriage and the Family, 39,* 587-599.

Nadelson, T., & Eisenberg, L. (1977). The successful professional woman: On being married to one. *American Journal of Psychiatry, 134,* 1071-1076.

Nettles, E. J., & Loevinger, J. (1983). Sex role expectations and ego level in relation to problem marriages. *Journal of Personality and Social Psychology, 45,* 676-687.

Nickols, S. Y., & Metzen, E. J. (1978). Impact of wife's employment upon husband's housework. *Journal of Family Issues, 3,* 199-216.

Oakley, A. (1974). *The sociology of housework*. New York: Pantheon.

Orden, S. R., & Bradburn, N. M. (1963). Working wives and marriage happiness. *American Journal of Sociology, 74,* 391-407.

Osherson, S., & Dill, D. (1983). Varying work and family choices: Their impact on men's work satisfaction. *Journal of Marriage and the Family, 45,* 339-346.

Osmond, M. W., & Martin, P. Y. (1975). Sex and sexism: A comparison of male and female sex-role attitudes. *Journal of Marriage and the Family, 37,* 744-758.

Papanek, H. (1973). Men, women, and work: Reflections on the two-person career. *American Journal of Sociology, 78,* 852-872.

Parsons, T. (1940). An analytical approach to the theory of social stratification. *American Journal of Sociology, 45,* 841-862.

Parsons, T. (1942). Age and sex in the social structure of the United States. *American Sociological Review, 7,* 604-616.

Parsons, T., & Bales, R. F. (1955). *Family, socialization, and interaction process*. Glencoe, IL: The Free Press.

Pearlin, L. (1975). Status inequality and stress in marriage. *American Sociological Review, 40,* 344-357.

Perucci, C., Potter, H., & Rhoads, D. (1978). Determinants of male family-role performance. *Psychology of Women Quarterly, 3,* 153-166.

Philliber, W. W., & Hiller, D. V. (1983). Relative occupational attainments of spouses and later changes in marriage and wife's work experience. *Journal of Marriage and the Family, 45,* 161-170.

Pleck, J. H. (1977). The work-family role system. *Social Problems, 24,* 417-427.

Pleck, J. H. (1978). *Men's new roles in the family*. Unpublished manuscript, Wellesley College Center for Research on Women, Wellesley, MA.

Poloma, M. M. (1972). Role conflict and the married professional woman. In C. Safilios-

Rothschild (Ed.), *Toward a sociology of women* (pp. 187-198). Lexington, MA: Xerox.

Poloma, M. M., & Garland, N. T. (1971). The married professional woman: A study in the tolerance of domestication. *Journal of Marriage and the Family, 33*, 531-540.

Poloma, M. M., Pendleton, B. F., & Garland, N. T. (1982). Reconsidering the dual-career marriage: A longitudinal approach. In J. Aldous (Ed.), *Two paychecks: Life in dual-earner families* (pp. 173-192). Beverly Hills, CA: Sage.

Poor, R. (Ed.). (1972). *4 days, 40 hours: Reporting a revolution in work and leisure.* London: Pan Books.

Rapoport, R., & Rapoport, R. N. (1969). The dual-career family: A variant pattern and social change. *Human Relations, 22*, 3-30.

Rapoport, R., & Rapoport, R. N. (1971). *Dual-career families.* Baltimore: Penguin.

Rapoport, R., & Rapoport, R. N. (1975). Men, women, and equity. *The Family Coordinator, 24*, 421-432.

Rapoport, R., & Rapoport, R. N. (1976). *Dual-career families re-examined.* London: Martin Robertson.

Rice, D. G. (1979). *Dual-career marriage: Conflict and treatment.* New York: The Free Press.

Richardson, J. G. (1979). Wife occupational superiority and marital status: An examination of the hypothesis. *Journal of Marriage and the Family, 41*, 63-72.

Robinson, J. (1977). *How Americans use their time.* New York: Praeger.

Rose, P. (1984). *Parallel lives: Five Victorian marriages.* New York: Knopf.

Rosenfield, S. (1980). Sex differences in depression: Do women always have higher rates? *Journal of Health and Social Behavior, 21*, 33-42.

Rosow, I., & Rose, D. K. (1972). Divorce among doctors. *Journal of Marriage and the Family, 32*, 587-598.

Ross, C. E., Mirowsky, J., & Huber, J. (1983). Dividing work, sharing work, and in-between: Marriage patterns and depression. *American Sociological Review, 48*, 809-823.

Ross, H. L., & Sawhill, I. V. (1975). *Time of transition.* Washington, DC: Urban Institute.

Rossi, A. (1965). Barriers to the career choice of engineering, medicine, or science among American women. In J. A. Mattfeld & C. G. VanAken (Eds.), *Women and the scientific professions* (pp. 51-127). Cambridge, MA: Massachusetts Institute of Technology Press.

Rubin, L. (1983). *Intimate strangers.* New York: Harper & Row.

Safilios-Rothschild, C., & Dijkers, (1978). Handling unconventional asymmetries. In R. Rapoport & R. Rapoport (Eds.), *Working couples* (pp. 62–73). New York: Harper & Row.

St. John-Parsons, D. (1978). Continuous dual-career families: A case study. *Psychology of Women Quarterly, 3*, 30-42.

Scanzoni, J. (1979). Social processes and power in families. In W. R. Burr, R. Hill, F. I. Nye, & I. L. Reiss (Eds.), *Contemporary theories about the family* (Vol. 1, pp. 295-316). New York: The Free Press.

Sekaran, U. (1983). Factors influencing the quality of life in dual-career families. *Journal of Occupational Psychology, 6*, 161-174.

Simpson, I. H., & England, P. (1981). Conjugal work roles and marital solidarity. *Journal of Family Issues, 2*, 180-204.

Spence, J. T. (1985). Gender identity and its implications for the concept of masculinity and femininity. In T. B. Sonderegger (Ed.), *Nebraska Symposium on Motivation: Vol. 32. Psychology and gender* (pp. 59-95). Lincoln: University of Nebraska Press.

Staines, G. L., Pleck, J. H., Shepard, L. J., & O'Connor, P. (1978). Wives' employment status and marital adjustment: Yet another look. *Psychology of Women Quarterly, 3*, 90-99.

Stewart, A. J. (1987, April). *Some consequences of the things our mothers didn't teach us: Social and individual change in women's lives*. Paper presented at the Eastern Psychological Association, Washington, DC.

Stewart, A. J., & Malley, J. E. (1987). Role combination in women in the early adult years: Mitigating agency and communion. In F. J. Crosby (Ed.), *Spouse, parent, worker: On gender and multiple roles* (pp. 44-62). New Haven, CT: Yale University Press.

Thoits, P. (1987). Negotiating roles. In F. J. Crosby (Ed.), *Spouse, parent, worker: On gender and multiple roles* (pp. 11-22). New Haven, CT: Yale University Press.

United States Department of Education. (1985). *Earned degrees conferred (annual)*. Washington, DC: Center for Statistics.

United States Department of Labor. (1985). *Labor force activity of mothers with young children continues at record pace* (Publication No. USDL 85-381). Washington, DC: Bureau of Labor Statistics.

Walker, K., & Woods, M. (1976). *Time use: A measure of household production of goods and services*. Washington, DC: American Home Economics.

Wallston, B. S., Foster, M. A., & Berger, M. (1978). I will follow him: Myth, reality or forced choice—Job-seeking experiences of dual-career couples. *Psychology of Women Quarterly, 3*, 9-21.

Weingarten, K. (1978). The employment pattern of professional couples and their distribution of involvement in the family. *Psychology of Women Quarterly, 3*, 43-52.

Weiss, R. S. (1985). Men and the family. *Family Process, 24*, 49-58.

Yankelovich, D. (1974). The meaning of work. In J. M. Rosow (Ed.), *The worker and the job* (pp. 19-47). Englewood Cliffs, NJ: Prentice Hall.

Yogev, S. (1981). Do professional women have egalitarian marital relationships? *Journal of Marriage and the Family, 43*, 865-871.

Young, M., & Willmott, P. (1973). *The symmetrical family*. New York: Pantheon.

Author Index

Subject Index